SCINTILLA
23

SUBSCRIPTIONS

All issues from SCINTILLA 16 onward can be purchased through Amazon.com or Amazon.co.uk. For convenience, we hope to make back issues available through Amazon in future. Issues 1-15 are available directly from The Vaughan Association. Please email subscriptions@vaughanassociation.org to get further details.

*

WEBSITE

www.vaughanassociation.org

EMAIL

subscriptions@vaughanassociation.org

Submissions for Scintilla 24

Please submit critical articles on literature in the metaphysical tradition to prose@vaughanassociation.org.

Please submit new poetry for consideration through the poetry submission portal on our website: http://www.vaughanassociation.org/submissions-to-scintilla/

All submissions are peer reviewed

SCINTILLA
The Journal of the Vaughan Association

23

'But life is, what none can express,
A quickness, which my God hath kist.'
Henry Vaughan 'Quickness'

'The Fields ... are green with the Breath of God,
and fresh with the Powers of Heaven.'
Thomas Vaughan, *Anima Magica Abscondita*

A journal of literary criticism, prose and new poetry
in the metaphysical tradition

Published by
The Vaughan Association

© Copyright remains with the author

Published in 2020
Scintilla is a publication of The Vaughan Association

Essays in each issue of *Scintilla* frequently originate in talks first given at The Vaughan Association's annual Colloquium held each spring near the Vaughans' birth-place at Newton Farm near Llansantffraed, Breconshire.

All rights reserved. No part of this publication may be reproduced, stored in a retrieval system, or transmitted, in any form or by any means, electronic, mechanical, photocopying, recording or otherwise, without the prior permission of The Vaughan Association.

ISBN: 9798646595721
ISSN 1368-5023

Published with the financial support of the Welsh Books Council
General Editor, Joseph Sterrett
Poetry Editors, Damian Walford Davies
and Kathrine Stanfield
Prose Editor, Erik Ankerberg
Reviews Editor, Elizabeth Ford
Assistant to General Editor, Christa Rydeberg Aakær

Editorial Board:
Alan Rudrum
Donald Dickson
Helen Wilcox
Robert Wilcher

Advisors:
John Barnie, Robert Minhinnick, M. Wynn Thomas

Art Work:
Anne Lewis
Printed by Kindle Direct Publishing

CONTENTS

Preface..5

Peter Pike	'Rending the veil of the usual': grace conveyed through the 'slightest things' in the poetry of Henry Vaughan.......... 9
Frances-Anne King	Balnakeil 32
Charles Wilkinson	'brumeux'... 33
Bruce Mcrae	The Hive's Heart 34
Peter Limbrick	Poet 35
	It was a short meeting 36
Thor Bacon	Isölte & Tristan 37
John Welch	Gardening 38
	Someone 40
Edmund Matyjaszek	A Crocus Field 41
Carol Barbour	Althernal Walk 42
Linda Black	Rails of dresses 43
Patrick Bond	The Bone Room 44
Shanta Acharya	Snowy Egret 45
	In Silence 46
Noel Canin	Memories and Ashes 48
Clare Crossman	The Territory of Water..................... 49
Tony Brown	'Sharing in the building': The Creative Relationship of R.S. Thomas and Elsi Eldridge 51
Claire Crowther	The Physics of Coincidence 86
	Confusional in a Gothic Church........ 87
Neil Curry	Sinai 88

Sam Davidson	Möbius 89
Holly Day	Escalation 90
Marek Urbanowicz	Lake Semerwater 91
Anna Flemming	Not a mountain 93
Robin Ford	What You Don't See When You Look At Me 94
Brigid Sivill	Rishi Valley 96
Christopher Meredith	Sound of leaves not falling 97
	Upstairs 98
Roger Garfitt	The Assyrian Moth 100
Sam Garvan	Tumulus 102
Davide Trame	What the Thunders Say 103
	The Sacred 104
Tom Gouthwaite	A Wish Unmeasured 105
	Zac's Oak 107
Holly Faith Nelson	Transatlantic Vaughan: The Afterlife of the Silurist in Early American Periodicals 108
Martin Hayden	A Journey to Make, Sometime 132
Martin Bennett	Alrewas Return 134
	Trent-Mersey Canal 135
Michael Henry	Pyromania 136
	Sunny Sands Tribute 137
Ric Hool	Enlightenment 138
	Halfway to Everything 139
Sarah Lindon	East 140
	Like Day and Night, Emerge and Hide 142
Sean H. Mcdowell	Photogram 144
	Three Lost Objects Found 148
Nicholas Mcgaughey	The Ring 149
William Virgil Davis	For Marie Curie on her 150th Birthday 150

	Widow 151
Claire Scott	Foundering 152
Paul Matthews	World Rose 153
	Winter Traces 154
Nicholas Murray	Parbold 155
	Europe 156
	A Short History of Ethics 158
Andrew Neilson	The Week's Remains 159
Susan Skinner	December Night at the Stable 161
	On a Beach 162
Jeremy Hooker	Under the Quarry Woods: journal into prose poetry 163
Jill Townsend	Waiting for Results 183
	Recovering 184
Robert Nisbet	The Archaeologists 185
Ann Pilling	After the Funeral 187
Mark Harshman	Mariners 188
Martin Potter	Walking the Old Beat 189
	Contemplate the Floor 190
Ranajit Sarkar	The Bran-Tub 191
Thomas R. Smith	The Library of Heaven 192
	Palm Sunday 193
Alex Barr	Iain 194
Kenneth Steven	Finally 196
	At Pluscarden Abbey 197
Beatrice Teissier	Jacques at the Solstice 198
	Cremation Day 199
	Signal 200
Hubert Moore	Back-licking 201
Denni Turp	System Incompatibility 202
Christine Valters Painter	Beloved 203

Donald R. Dickson	Henry Vaughan, Scholarly Editor 204
Mike Jenkins	Back With the Smoke 246
Dominic Weston	Ghost of a flea 247
	It's just You and Me Now 249
Isabel Bermudez	Winter Vines 251
Margaret Wilmot	Chandeliers 252
	Seasonal Variation on a Railway Platform 254
Chris Dodd	The Field 255
Sam Adams	from 'Notes of an Interview with Michel Eyquem, Seigneur De Montaine' 256
Jonathan Wooding	from 'Force' 257
K.E. Duffin	Visitation at Newport 258
Rosie Jackson	Resurrection 259
	After the Door has Opened 260
Frank Dullaghan	Skull 262
Kevin Cahill	Lao Tzu has a Go 263
Patrick Deeley	Dream of a Fallen Beast 264
	Rigour 266
Miles Parker	Luggala 1982 268
B.J. Buckley	Music for the Third Ear 269
Linda Saunders	My Mother Being Very Deaf 271
Rosie Jackson	Resurrection 274
	After the Door has Opened 275
Philip West	Review: The Works of Henry Vaughan 276

Contributors 281

Preface

Scintilla began, and continues to be, an extended, ongoing conversation about the legacy, interests, and experience of the Vaughan brothers. These identical twins, Thomas, an alchemist, and Henry, the poet, never forgot the beauty of their Breaconshire countryside and continually returned to their memories of the Usk river valley, its gently rolling hills, dense groves, flowers, trees, rock outcrops, rivers, history and myths. It is this landscape that infuses their work and remained an imaginative stronghold as the social and political world transformed around them, very often as a result of violence. England and Wales in the seventeenth century experienced the horror of civil war, transforming and frequently erasing familiar political and religious institutions. This bewildering time is a profound presence in their work, the struggle to retain identity and continuity when so many things that ought to provide solidity were in meltdown. Henry and Thomas both responded creatively, reinventing themselves, Henry as 'Silurist' and Thomas as 'Eugenius Philalethes'. Their work traces the creative process in relation to identity and adversity, probing the intersections between them, the past and present, a sense of place, its physical environment, and a vision of one's inner life. It employs the language of metaphysical experience, questioning, poetry and healing as well as the concrete searching of science.

Scintilla 23 turns our attention to the creative impulses that shaped Henry's thinking and were shaped by him. Peter Pike opens this issue with a fascinating discussion of the legacy of Vaughan's attention to the 'slightest things', a poetic concentration that carries 'a charge which has contributed to the grace of subsequent writing in English'. Reading Vaughan's, 'Thou that know'st for whom I mourn', Pike traces a similar poetic attention through later poets including John Clare, Edward Thomas, Ted Hughes, and Kathleen Jamie.

Donald Dickson examines Henry Vaughan as a scholarly editor, sleuthing the patristic, classical, and contemporary sources that Henry had at his disposal or where he might have had access to them. Examining the sketchy records from libraries and their users in the seventeenth century, Dickson explores how much can be gleaned from this surprisingly rich, if challenging intellectual environment. It is likely, Dickson asserts, that Vaughan had a surprising number of his sources in his own personal library, a point consistent with what was known to be his considerable collection of medical texts. It also seems that Vaughan improved 'his school boy' Greek and German as he matured, giving us a much stronger picture of the poet-physician's intellectual life.

Holly Nelson extends our view of Vaughan, examining the transcontinental reception in 19th-century North America. Vaughan's poetry, having almost disappeared from a reading public in the 18th century, seems to have met a need in the moralistic religious American culture of the 19th. The need was often quite removed from Vaughan's context. His political undertones were frequently erased, his spiritual specificity universalised and sentimentalised. Commenting on the end of 'As time one day by me did pass', Nelson notes, 'One can imagine voracious consumers of Charles Dickens's novels in Britain and America (devastated by the death of Little Nell in The Old Curiosity Shop) sentimentalizing and universalizing the substance of Vaughan's pilcrowed poems, rather than focusing on the historical reality of war and death that contributed to the elegiac idiom of such lines'. Yet, it was such readers who paved the way for those who would engage more fully with the Silurist's work, like Louise Imogen Guiney whose unfinished research would provide the basis for F.E. Hutchinson's 20th-century reappraisal.

Tony Brown expands an abiding interest of Scintilla into the life and poetry of R.S. Thomas, unfolding the story of his artistic wife, Elsi, and crediting her as a significant influence, training and inspiring him in a life of 'looking', deeply, at the world around him. Brown shows examples of Elsi's 'looking', not least her looking at her husband, carefully transposed to the paper through her drawings. These images juxtapose and illustrate Thomas's poems, and the two give us a sense of their creative marriage over so many years.

Jeremy Hooker gives us a personal insight into his own writing process, particularly his experience involved in writing prose poems over the years. Hooker ties the prose poem to the practice of keeping a daily journal; he sees the act of bringing those two forms together as a movement toward self-knowledge for the poet. In this act, the poet's text becomes a kind of 'quarry' that the poet pursues and forms into a 'made thing' or a 'shape in words.'

Scintilla continues to offer a space for contemporary poetry written in necessarily complex dialogue with the tradition of the Vaughan brothers. In doing so, we bring together, once more, established writers and new voices. One such new voice is American poet Emily Crispino, a graduate student in archival science with an interest in the life and writings of the Vaughan brothers. Her sparkling poem 'For Thomas and Rebecca Vaughan' is included in this issue. Crispino's poem and the rest of the work chosen for this issue were not only written before the advent of COVID-19 but also selected before this point too, and the poems now seem like missives from another world. As with all good poetry that prompts thought, they speak to us from another time and do so with relevance for the challenging circumstances in which we look to make sense of things unutterable and unmatched. Crispino speaks of the 'whisper of bodies split and knit, / of spirits magnetized / by nature's flame and firmament'. At a time of social distancing, we have all been split but are learning to knit anew, in new ways.

Andrew Neilson's poem 'The Week's Remains' celebrates the end-of-the-week drink as a chance to take stock. The poem asks: 'How long can luck last?'. With 'an eye applied to a telescope lens' we can stare down the vista of all possible disasters and count our blessings even as we acknowledge the suffering of others. Now, in the midst of one such disaster, an end-of-the-week drink with friends and colleagues might seem a far-off event for many. As a result, we're likely to turn inward. Shanta Acharya's ghazal 'In Silence' assures us, however, that we will find that 'love's a patch of green that flowers in silence – / a shade that shelters you in times of crises, / a place you keep returning to in silence.'

'Rending the veil of the usual': grace conveyed through the 'slightest things' in the poetry of Henry Vaughan

PETER PIKE

In his collection *Station Island* (1984), Seamus Heaney, in the persona of Sweeney, the bird-king exiled to the canopy of trees, acknowledges the traits of his fellow species, including 'the unbegrudging concentration / of the heron' and 'the allure of the cuckoo'. He continues:

> But when goldfinch or kingfisher rent
> the veil of the usual,
> pinions whispered and braced
>
> as I stooped, unwieldy
> and brimming,
> my spurs at the ready.[1]

Any other world there may be, glanced momentarily through the flash of a bird, presses upon, and breathes within, this familiar one. It is reachable through a tear in the thinnest of fabrics, a notion consistent with the Celtic perception of heaven being 'just six feet above our heads'. Sweeney, about to take flight in pursuit of this place of elusive yet earthed magic, is 'unwieldy / and brimming'. He is conscious that he is both unprepared for the task while also being filled with an unquantifiable hope.

---

[1] 'Drifting Off', *Station Island* (London: Faber, 1984), pp. 104-5.

This paper follows Sweeney's pursuit. It is stimulated by an aspect of Henry Vaughan's poetry which offers readers the 'ordinary', the 'slightest things'. The argument runs that such things, when attended to closely, carry a charge which has contributed to the grace of subsequent writing in English. It also argues that, dwelling on these 'slightest things', allowing them, as it were, to speak, is also crucial for the reception and expression of faith for Anglicans (as Vaughan was) in contemporary Wales. These two strands have strong mutual elements.

A close reading of Vaughan's works reveals a poet searching himself, and nature, with a palette drawn towards the light, which is sometimes angelic and full, sometimes intuited at depth, and sometimes dim and sorrowful, as if hutched in by darkness.[2]

Vaughan's dynamics of light are noted by Rowan Williams. For him, the poet shared,

> with the entire Platonist and Hermetic world of his day, the conviction that there was a consonance and mutual attraction between what was above and what was below: so the light of the stars is drawn towards us and we are drawn up to and into it.[3]

Fixing Vaughan's work in a stable frame is slippery. For Thomas Calhoun, '(l)iterary criticism alone cannot dispel the confusion about Vaughan's Hermeticism.'[4] Vaughan's worldview, although steeped in the early Anglican Augustinian, even

---

[2] See, for example, Rembrandt's *The Entombment of Christ*.
[3] Rowan Williams, 'Reflections on the Vaughan Brothers: Poetry meets Metaphysics', *Scintilla*, 21 (2018), p. 13.
[4] Thomas Calhoun, *Henry Vaughan: The Achievement of Silex Scintillans* (East Brunswick, London, Toronto: Associated University Presses, 1981), pp. 112-3.

Calvinist, ethos, explored so realistically by George Herbert, was also strongly syncretist, and open to what some of his contemporaries would have regarded as dangerous speculation. The nuances of this, so central to his and Thomas's life and faith in the Usk valley, are difficult to comprehend fully today. What is clear is that the presence of light and its paradoxical existence in darkness irradiate Vaughan's poetry and are its hallmark.

Vaughan's poem *'Thou that know'st for whom I mourn'* inevitably issues from an hermetic perception of the cosmos. The poem is read with some hermeneutical risk, bearing this in mind, but choosing primarily to focus on some of the objects to be found in it.

Initially, Vaughan explains to the Lord that the gift of tears on his brother William's death could easily have been prevented if his sibling had been granted a longer life. He then argues, somewhat tendentiously, that his own sin precipitated his younger brother's demise, which death could even be understood as for his benefit, as a writer.

About a third of the way through the poem is a brief inventory of discarded objects which is the catalyst for this paper:

> Nine months thy hands are fashioning us,
> And many years (alas!)
> Ere we can lisp, or aught discuss
> Concerning thee, must pass;
> Yet I have known thy slightest things
> A *feather*, or a *shell*,
> A *stick*, or *rod* which some chance brings
> The best of us excel,
> Yea, I have known these shreds out last
> A fair-compacted frame

'Rending the veil of the usual'

> And for one *twenty* we have passed
> Almost outlive our name.[5]

A feather, a shell, a stick and a rod lie, powered down in the architecture of the poem, but obstinate in themselves and capable of conveying poetic and theological grace beyond that structure. Vaughan's eye also rests on, and attends to, potentially disregarded 'everyday' things in other poems. For example, in the third stanza of 'The Bird', he notes that, although 'poor stones have neither speech nor tongue . . . Yet (they) are deep in admiration'.[6]

In the immediate context of *'Thou that know'st for whom I mourn'*, the 'chance' finds of the feather, shell, stick and rod are visible reminders of the observable finitude of death as distinct from the inwardness of heaven and 'close eternity'. For all their transience they are a more profitable stopping point in the poem than some of the conventional wisdoms about 'authentic' grief and the need to have knowledge of our end, if we are to share the 'same crown' as the late-lamented William. The writing shades disappointingly into an improving message, whereas a feather, a shell, a stick and a rod, left on the ground, mark the beginnings of a slender trail of grace. Vaughan's possessive pronoun is important, as '(y)et have I known *thy* slightest things' reveals that although such 'shreds' may be easily overlooked they are, nevertheless, gift.

In this paper, in the literary sense, grace approximates to a slender but tenacious legacy of close observation to be inherited from the work of others, and duly developed. Things thus attended to, yield themselves onto the page. A poet's concentration on what others may discount as the 'everyday'

---

[5] Alan Rudrum, ed., *Henry Vaughan: The Complete Poems* (Harmondsworth: Penguin, 1976), p. 170.
[6] Rudrum, 'The Bird', p. 261.

can be alchemic. Jonathan Bate offers a summary of Ted Hughes's capturing attention, especially in his writing for children but recognizable across his work:

> Think yourself into the moment. Touch, smell and listen to the thing you are writing about. Turn yourself into it. Then you will have it. That, for Hughes, was the essence of poetry.[7]

Attentiveness, whether to an object or an experience, has the potential to change the observer. Denise Levertov begins her poem 'O Taste and See':

> The world is
> not with us enough.
> *O taste and see*
>
> the subway Bible poster said,
> meaning *The Lord*, meaning
> if anything all that lives
> in the imagination's tongue,
>
> grief, mercy, language,
> tangerine, weather, to
> breathe them, bite,
> savour, chew, swallow, transform
>
> into our flesh our
> deaths . . . [8]

---

[7] Jonathan Bate, *Ted Hughes: The Unauthorised Life* (London: Collins, 2015), p. 45.
[8] Paul Lacey, ed., *Denise Levertov: New Selected Poems* (Tarset: Bloodaxe, 2003), p. 36.

The relishing of 'all that lives / in the imagination's tongue' gradually transforms people, and at levels of which they may be unaware. As Iris Murdoch wrote, 'Where virtue is concerned we often apprehend more than we clearly understand and *grow by looking*'.[9] Vaughan may be considered as a pioneer in this 'witnessing of the specific' in his writing, and Rowan Williams distinguishes him in this respect from George Herbert. For Williams, Vaughan 'is consistently someone who observes landscape' and, although he 'has none of Herbert's psychological acuity, his ear for the unexpected turns of speech . . . he makes up for it by his eye for the material environment.'[10]

There is no pure lineal descent from Vaughan's poetic close observation to subsequent writers in English, and this aspect of his craft is inevitably cross-bred with that of others. However, mention of three poets from the last couple of centuries who seemed 'to grow by looking', will lead to a more detailed consideration of one poem published in 2012, by Kathleen Jamie.

John Clare was first published two hundred years ago. His idiosyncratic work had many antecedents and influences, both aural and written, including the ballads heard during his youth and James Thomson's *The Seasons* (1730). As a boy 'he could 'get the whole book of Job by heart'',[11] and this can only have fuelled his appetite for seeing the detail in his surroundings. Job gives us, in the Authorized Version, 'the man whom God correcteth . . . shalt be in league with the stones of the field' (5:23); and the rhetorical question of the Lord to Job, 'Who

---

[9] Iris Murdoch, *The Sovereignty of Good* (London: Routledge & Kegan Paul, 1970), p. 31, italics in the original.
[10] Williams, p. 17.
[11] J. W. Tibble and Anne Tibble, eds, *John Clare: Selected Poems* (London: Dent, 1965), p.vii.

hath divided a watercourse for the overflowing of waters . . . (t)o satisfy the desolate and waste ground; and to cause the bud of the tender herb to spring forth?'(38:25a, 27).

Out birding, Clare spots at ground level the skylark's home. Here, Vaughan's casually cast sticks and rods have been gathered to make something simple and useful:

> Behind a clod how snug the nest
> Is in a horse's footing fixed!
> Of twitch and stubbles roughly dressed,
> With roots and horsehair intermixed.[12]

Clare's procedure of attending so closely to objects that he, in Hughes's term, turned himself into them, was essentially simple, leading to his frustration that 'Crowds see no magic in the trifling thing'.[13] His startling admission that he 'found the poems in the fields / And only wrote them down'[14] underscores both the concentration required and the nerve to yield unselfconsciously to an object's 'pull' so that it 'comes true' in the writing.

Clare's voice re-emerged, like a clump of perennials overlooked for seventy-five years or so, in the poetry of Edward Thomas, written from the outset of the First World War. Thomas reckoned, in his *The Tenth Muse* (1912), that there seemed 'no unbridged gulf' between Vaughan's early work 'and his sacred poems and pious thoughts and ejaculations'. However, 'what the change was that put the waterfall's murmurs and the flowers into eternity, and made the rain

---

[12] Tibble and Tibble, p. 215.
[13] Tibble and Tibble, p. 185.
[14] Found at: www.thelandmagazine.org.uk/articles/its-only-bondage-was-circling-sky-john-clare-and-enclosure-helpston

'Rending the veil of the usual'

visibly come from God's hand, we do not know . . .'[15] Thomas would have questioned Vaughan's personal possessive pronoun, '*thy* slightest things', although his attention to the sticks, feathers, shells and minutiae of his long-distance walks verified his contribution to this 'close observation' in poetry in English. He wrote on 18 March 1915:

> But these things also are Spring's –
>
> (. . .) The shell of a little snail bleached
> In the grass; chip of flint, and mite
> Of chalk, and the small birds' dung
> In splashes of purest white . . .[16]

Or, at the other end of the year, in dirty November weather, he noted that 'the prettiest things on the ground are the paths / With morning and evening hobnails dinted.' [17] Keeping his eyes to the ground, he observes, in 'After Rain', that

> The leaflets out of the ash-tree shed
> Are thinly spread
> In the road, like little black fish, inlaid . . .[18]

In his garden, touch and smell are drawn into the savouring of the 'hoar-green feathery herb' – Old Man – which stands as a whispering sentry outside the back door, as his daughter passes.

---

[15] Edward Thomas, *The Tenth Muse* (London: Martin Secker, 1912), p. 48.
[16] Edna Longley, ed., *Edward Thomas: The Annotated Collected Poems* (Tarset: Bloodaxe, 2008), p. 67.
[17] Longley, p. 34.
[18] Longley, p. 38.

In the eponymous poem, she pinches the leaves and sniffs her fingers, 'perhaps / Thinking, perhaps of nothing'.[19]

The poet, as adult, likewise confesses:

> I sniff the spray
> And think of nothing; I see and I hear nothing:
> Yet seem, too, to be listening, lying in wait
> For what I should, yet never can, remember.[20]

Here, the aroma of the simple shrub stimulates something remembered and perhaps, at the same time, mysteriously elusive to the writer and the reader. In Thomas's hands, Vaughan's 'slightest things' become catalysts for something else, with a range of reference beyond themselves.

Vaughan, in *'The Author's Preface to the Following Hymns'*, at the beginning of *Silex I*, establishes clearly a context of faith for his subsequent endeavours. He begs leave 'to communicate this my poor *talent* to the Church, under the *protection* and *conduct* of her *glorious Head* . . .'[21] Edward Thomas, in the trenches, abjured theological certainty of any kind as the framework for his writing but, in doing so, left his readers with an honest, deep agnosticism. The notes on the last pages of his diary, found on his body after his death, included what could be read as a moving *apologia* for prayer: 'I never understood quite what was meant by God.'[22]

To what extent has the grace of the 'legacy of close observation' in writing, mentioned earlier, grown in the century since Edward Thomas's death? In the following year, Robert

---

[19] Longley, p. 36.
[20] *Ibid*.
[21] Rudrum, p. 142.
[22] R George Thomas, ed., *Edward Thomas:The Collected Poems and War Diary, 1917* (London: Faber, 2004), p. 171.

'Rending the veil of the usual'

Bridges introduced the poetry of Gerard Manley Hopkins, with his flexing, microscopic eye, to the literary world.[23] 'In a flash, at a trumpet crash'[24] minute detail, sometimes refracted, arguably became a strong material for poetic fusion for subsequent writers to this day.

Henry Vaughan's 'stones . . . deep in admiration', take their place in a paean to that *Providence* where '(a)ll things that be, praise him'.[25] Moving on to the 1960s, a dimension in common between Henry Vaughan's poem 'The Bird' and Ted Hughes's poem 'Pibroch' is depth: in the first, stones are 'deep in admiration'; in the second, a stone, neutered by the wind, is deep in meaninglessness.

In a note provided about the title of his poem, Hughes wrote, '(a) Pibroch is a piece of music for bagpipes, a series of variations . . . including dirges'.[26] In Vaughan's poem, the stones, 'deep in admiration', invite personification which in turn connotes a degree of awe and even pleasurable contemplation. By contrast, Hughes' stone, hunkered down in interstellar darkness, shrugs off any element of heat and wind, or indeed, meaning:

> A pebble is imprisoned
> Like nothing in the Universe.
> Created for black sleep. Or growing
> Conscious of the sun's red spot occasionally,
> Then dreaming it is the foetus of God.

---

[23] In 1918 Bridges published a first collection of Hopkins's work.
[24] 'That Nature is a Heraclitean Fire and of the comfort of the Resurrection', W.H.Gardner and N.H.MacKenzie, eds., *The Poems of Gerard Manley Hopkins* 4th. edn. (Oxford: Oxford University Press, 1970), p. 105.
[25] Rudrum, p. 261.
[26] Paul Keegan, ed., *Ted Hughes: Collected Poems* (London: Faber, 2003), p. 1252.

The sea, '(p)robably bored with the appearance of heaven' and '(w)ithout purpose, without self-deception' and a tree – '(a)n old woman fallen from space' – complete the scene:

> Minute after minute, aeon after aeon,
> Nothing lets up or develops.
> And this is neither a bad variant nor a tryout.
> This is where the staring angels go through.
> This is where all the stars bow down.[27]

This is a dark counter-fugue to the Benedicite. All the works which 'bless the Lord' in that canticle are here stripped of their benevolent co-ordinates. The contention that this perpetual bleakness is 'neither a bad variant nor a tryout' reverses the first of the two accounts of creation in Genesis where 'God saw everything that he had made, and indeed, it was very good' (1:31).

'Pibroch' is bracing and allows no inherent sense of consolation 'in the way things are'. It is a chilling antidote to any facile recourse to arguments from design for creation. The challenge is for the crushed reader to resist any self-deception about the bleak, cold-shouldering universe being described. Yet the way in which the poem negates any qualities that might be attributable to God is itself a recognisable Christian tradition, that of negative or 'apophatic' theology. It is intriguing that the last two lines, with the angels and stars as mute agencies or onlookers of this impersonal stasis, are a faint echo of hermeticism.[28] Recognising an apophatic reading here allows

---

[27] Ted Hughes, *Wodwo* (London: Faber, 1967), p. 177.
[28] For Hughes's interest in Hermeticism see, for example, 'Shakespeare and Occult Neoplatonism', in William Scammell, ed., *Winter Pollen: Occasional Prose: Ted Hughes* (London: Faber, 1995), pp. 293-309.

'Rending the veil of the usual'

the radical questioning and augmenting of a provisional theology 'from a Christian perspective'.

With Kathleen Jamie's 'Materials', from her collection *The Overhaul* (2012), there is a distinct return to attending to Vaughan's 'slightest shreds' of things :

Materials

See when it all unravels – the entire project
reduced to threads of moss fleeing a nor'wester;
d'you ever imagine chasing just one strand, letting it lead
　you
to an unsung cleft in a rock, a place you could take to,
dig yourself in – but what are the chances of that?

Of the birds
few remain all winter; half a dozen waders
mediate between sea and shore, that space confirmed -
don't laugh – by your own work. Waves boom, off-white
spume-souls twirl out of geos, and look,

blown about the headland: scraps of nylon fishing net.
　Gannets
– did you know? – pluck such rubbish from the waves, then
　hie awa'
to colonies so raucous and thief-ridden, each nest
winds up swagged to the next . . . Then they're flown, and
　the
　　cliff's left
wearing naught but a shoddy, bird-knitted vest.

And look at us! Out all day and damn all to show for it.
Bird-bones, rope-scraps, a cursory sketch – but a bit o'
bruck's
all we need to get us started, all we'll leave behind us when
we're gone.[29]

In this poem, tresses of rubbish from a Scottish beach flit past readers' eyes, inviting them to 'imagine chasing one such strand' in the wind. This is an opportunity literally 'to pick up' an abandoned object which, remembering Vaughan, 'some chance brings', and follow its unravelling lead. This may be 'to an unsung cleft in the rock' or to a gannets' colony. The images along that quest are precise, as seen through a series of lifts of some binoculars: the scuttle of waders between the high and low water marks; spume; scraps of nylon fishing net; nests 'swagged' to each other; and the after-marks of the gannets' occupation of the cliff face – 'a shoddy, bird-knitted vest'.

The poem is as conversational as Vaughan's *'Thou that know'st for whom I mourn'* but in a different way. Vaughan's exchanges with the Lord and the reader are rhetorical and formal, whereas Jamie's are colloquial: 'd'you ever imagine?', 'but what are the chances of that?' and 'did you know?' The poem seems less knowing about what it might be up to than Vaughan's, and strangely at home in the wind-blown ephemera compared with Hughes's impersonal threnody. The activity of beachcombing in the wind is shared and recognizable by most readers, but the 'issue', which it wears very lightly, is no less universal. The reflective pause at the conclusion of the poem is both as slight and strong as a piece of discarded nylon rope: 'a bit o' bruck's / all we need to get us started, all we'll leave behind us when / we're gone'.

---

[29] Kathleen Jamie, *The Overhaul* (London: Picador, 2012), p. 50.

The journalist, Kirsty Scott, interviewed Jamie nearly fifteen years ago and wrote:

> She hopes her work is spiritual, a role she thinks writers can and should play, but she is not religious, having 'lost all patience' with Christianity and other monotheistic beliefs . . . (W)hen Phil (her husband) fell ill, (a) friend asked if she had prayed. She hadn't. But she had done what she does best. 'I had noticed', she writes in 'Fever', 'the cobwebs and the shoaling light and the way the doctor listened and the flecked tweed of her skirt . . . Isn't that a kind of prayer? The care and maintenance of the web of our noticing, the paying heed?[30]

*

The word 'grace' is more recognizable in a devotional context. The fruits of Vaughan's celebration of, and struggle with, faith, as described in his work, may likewise be conveyed or transmitted through time as 'gift'. This is enriching for the current reader from the same denomination. It offers profound insights on 'keeping the ground' if or when – as Vaughan counselled his co-religionists in 'Rules and Lessons' – '*priest*, and *people* change'.[31] This was vital advice in the early 1650s when, the 'native expression of Christian doctrine, the Church of England's Prayer Book, had been cut in pieces with a pen-

---

[30] Kirsty Scott, 'In the nature of things', based on an Interview with Kathleen Jamie, 'Review of Books', *Guardian*, 18 June 2005 at:
www.theguardian.com/books/2005/jun/18/featuresreviews.guardianreview15
[31] Rudrum, p. 193.

knife, and thrown into the fire',[32] and livings, including Thomas Vaughan's, were lost. Such dislocation and discontinuity is not part of Anglican experience today, although some closing of buildings and re-grouping of parishes into ministry or mission areas continues to be challenging. In the middle of all this, there is a need to re-emphasize imagination as a crucial element in the reception and expression of faith. Reading Vaughan confirms this and, as Stevie Davies notes, his 'nature poetry suggests a new beatitude: "Blessed are the imaginative for they already see God."'[33] The grace conveyed from Henry Vaughan's attention to the 'slightest things' in his writing re-iterates the unobtrusive but vital place of attentive imagination at the heart of the collective endeavour of the church, resourcing it and even, on occasions, subverting it.

The writer has recently retired from stipendiary ordained ministry after thirty-five years in the Church of England and, latterly, in the Church in Wales; which are, respectively, Henry Vaughan's nurturing church and, for the last one hundred years, its particular Welsh expression. The brief connections and comments which follow are offered in appreciation of former colleagues' continuing commitment to its life and witness.

Change has been exponential, including radically altering understandings of what it means to be a human being, of the nature of the sources of faith, and the place of biblical writings in the formulation of doctrine and practice alongside or within different cultures' self-expressions.

---

[32] Reggie Askew, *Muskets and Altars: Jeremy Taylor and the Last of the Anglicans* (London: Mowbray, 1997), p. 2. In this context the sentiment applies to Jeremy Taylor but it is equally true of Henry Vaughan.
[33] Stevie Davies, *Henry Vaughan* (Bridgend: Seren, 1995), p. 134.

'Rending the veil of the usual'

Thus far, attention to Vaughan's 'slightest' feather, shell, stick or rod have yielded Clare's closeness to the earth, his *humus* or humility; Edward Thomas's agnosticism about any meta-source for his bleached shell in the grass; Ted Hughes's implacable showing of a universe where 'nothing lets up or develops', which may also be read as the stirrings of a 'negative' theology; and Kathleen Jamie's alert and tentative approach to prayer as '(t)he care and web of our noticing, the paying heed'.

These glimpses into the imagination working on simple objects already suggest lines of development for the contemporary renewing of prayer and expressions of belief. Within them is licence to deconstruct certainty and resurrect the vitality of doubt as a part of faith. Vaughan's work enables this through the range of his imagination, first, stimulated by his inhabiting biblical passages; second, by his understanding of 'first things' being as critical as 'last things' in any life's evaluation; and third by an honesty about death which potentially deepens and makes more realistic a sensitive funeral ministry.

Vaughan's poems are steeped in biblical narratives, with their touchstone often being a biblical text. Taking just one example, 'The Night' draws on many biblical references beyond that which is declared below its title – 'John iii 2', or the coming of Nicodemus to Christ by night. Also included within the poem are '(t)hat sacred veil' (Hebrews 10:32), 'the long expected healing wings' (Malachi 4:2), the 'mercy-seat of gold' (Exodus 37:6), '*Christ's* . . . prayer time (Mark 1:35, Luke 21:37), and, more generally, Christ in the wilderness (Mark 1:12, 13 and parallels).

Not knowing Vaughan's procedures as a poet, it is difficult to assess whether the text that we now have emerged from a clearly-conceived structure, or whether some of the details to be found in it were the first catalysts for its existence. It may well have been a combination of both. The form of the argument is fairly clear: Nicodemus sees sufficiently to 'know his God' by moonlight, and, although the place of encounter is tantalizingly unknown, it is among the Lord's 'living works' rather than in previous cultic places of disclosure. The 'Calm and unhaunted' night is preferable to daylight's delusions, and God's 'deep but dazzling darkness' is where the poet desires to live 'invisible and dim'.

Conversely, the poem may have started from Vaughan 'paying heed' to some of the details which were eventually included in it; his recollection of the moonlight's effects, a rare flower on a cushion of leaves, and locks of hair, drenched by dew, with these being his 'threading points' as the poem progressed.[34]

Vaughan's deeply imaginative playfulness with the biblical account of the meeting between Nicodemus and Christ both unsettles and augments subsequent doctrine, giving the reader a God of '(some say) / . . . deep but dazzling darkness'. Rather than reckoning that the text serves as a building block for a doctrinal construction (in this case, the necessity of 'being born again') it should be read with as little preconception as possible, letting individual details resonate. Taking into account the insights of biblical criticism and what others have made of the text, someone reading with devotional intent needs to be imaginatively receptive to its associations, 'lying in wait / For what (they) should, yet never can, remember' (Edward Thomas). Vaughan's work provides a very rich vein of biblical passages worked on imaginatively in this way.

---

[34] Such attention to detail, expanding to narrative, can also be found in Pasolini's film *The Gospel According to St Matthew* (1964) with its sparse, particular camera work, and people and panoramas as seen through the eyes of Christ. Part of the film's soundtrack is Blind Willie Johnson's 'Dark was the night, cold was the ground', and the haunting, wordless melody could almost serve as an accompaniment to Vaughan's poem.

'Rending the veil of the usual'

Another pervasive source for Vaughan's writing was his childhood, his 'Angel-infancy', before he 'taught (his) tongue to wound / (his) conscience with a sinful sound', and where he 'felt through all this fleshly dress / Bright *shoots* of everlastingness'.[35] This may not be a universal early-years experience, as some childhoods are more fractured and troubled than Vaughan's. But a looking back, with a careful re-entry to this fledgling landscape, where all is believable, is a corrective to an understanding of faith comprised solely of an adult existential decision, or of decades of religious practice, and may open up quite different perspectives on present experience.

'The Evening Watch' is a dialogue between the body and the soul, where the latter enjoins the former to 'sleep in peace . . . Unnumbered in thy dust'.[36] The body accepts this challenging counsel but asks, before they both part, how long it is until the day of God's final reconciliation. The soul reassures the about-to-be-bereft body; 'who drew this circle even / He fills it . . . Yet, this take with thee; the last gasp of time / Is thy first breath, and man's *eternal prime*.'[37]

This return to the profound significance of beginnings recurs in writing in English, through Wordsworth, on to Seamus Heaney. In the Irish poet's 'Mint', that rampant herb is relished,

> (a)s if something callow yet tenacious
> Sauntered in green alleys and grew rife.
>
> The snip of scissor blades, the light of Sunday
> Mornings when the mint was cut and loved:

---

[35] *'The Retreat'*, Rudrum, pp. 172-3.
[36] *'The Evening Watch'*, Rudrum, p. 180.
[37] *Ibid.*

> My last things will be first things slipping from me.
> Yet let all things go free that have survived.[38]

Heaney the poet recognizes that all that was accumulating in the fragrant domestic circle of his early years may actually comprise what are more often anticipated as dramatic 'last things'. This insight is released as quietly, and almost insubstantially, as the fading aroma of mint boiling with the new potatoes.

Attentive imagination to what we have already experienced is a form of 'care and maintenance of the web of our noticing', a form of prayer. With 'the grace of accuracy'[39] rather than an indulgent nostalgia, this could deepen the vitality of the church's collective expression of faith.

The final lines of Vaughan's *'The Retreat'* provide a bridge to the last 'slightest thing', and perhaps the least substantial of all: mortal dust. The poem concludes:

> Some men a forward motion love,
> But I by backward steps would move,
> And when this dust falls to the urn
> In that state I came return.[40]

Contemplation of Vaughan's younger brother's remains haunts his verse, and *'Silence and stealth of days'* is an extended treatment of this. The poet is precise: it is '(t)welve hundred hours' between the time of writing and the fatal event, and he retraces his steps backwards 'o'er fled minutes . . . / Unto that

---

[38] Seamus Heaney, *The Spirit Level* (London: Faber, 1996), p. 6.
[39] 'Epilogue', Frank Bidart and David Gewanter, eds., *Robert Lowell: Collected Poems* (London: Faber, 2003), p. 838.
[40] Rudrum, p. 173.

hour'.[41] The journey is desolate, and although Vaughan concedes a vivifying light where 'those fled to their Maker's throne, / There shine, and burn',[42] the poem cannot quite escape the gravitational pull of finitude. William is gone, his mortal dust reducing fast, and at the core of this constriction, Vaughan writes:

> Yet I have one *pearl* by whose light
> All things I see,
> And in the heart of earth, and night
> Find Heaven, and thee.'[43]

This gift cannot be presumed and needs daily rediscovery. If it is the pearl of great price its appropriation costs 'not less than everything',[44] revealing that a hope in the meaning of our lives, hidden in the life, death and resurrection of Jesus Christ, although gift, is equally hard-won. Applying this when alongside the families of the bereaved requires pastoral tact and sensitivity. Attempting to distil the essence of what is being shared about the deceased person, to inform honest thanksgiving and commendation, needs perseverance, and the readiness to take risks. Vaughan's honesty is a fortifier here.

At the conclusion of '*I walked the other day*', Vaughan asks to be led 'above', that the Lord might show him William's 'life again / At whose dumb urn / Thus all the year I mourn'.[45] The poet again seems tethered to these insubstantial remains. But the very state of dust may prove eloquent. Part of the third stanza of 'Burial' reads:

---

[41] Rudrum, pp. 180-1.
[42] *Ibid*.
[43] *Ibid*.
[44] See T.S. Eliot's 'Little Gidding', *Collected Poems: 1909–1962* (London: Faber, 1963), p. 223.
[45] Rudrum, p. 242.

> Thou art the same, faithful, and just
> In life, or dust;
> Though then (thus crumbed) I stray
> In blasts,
> Or exhalations, and wastes
> Beyond all eyes
> Yet thy love spies
> That change, and knows thy clay.[46]

Another Welsh poet, Vernon Watkins, restates well this finely tuned balance between a vapid hope for the heavenly realms and a denial of any life's meaning:

> For every argument but the silent prayer of the dust itself, expecting resurrection, is an evasion of the truth, swayed by a too optimistic hope or a too impatient despair from its true music.[47]

Vaughan's readiness to lament without recourse to formulaic consolation runs a steel core through much of today's rather diffuse language surrounding grief and loss. It offers a narrow path through unfitting sentimentality and refuge in barely believed doctrinal certainties. Savouring this insight of Vaughan's potentially breathes new life into a eulogy where some of the nuanced detail of the life of the departed may be set alongside, and interact with, the imaginative probing of a biblical passage.

---

[46] Rudrum, p. 183.
[47] Vernon Watkins, *The Death Bell* (London: Faber, 1954), p. 111.

Another paper awaits a more extensive appreciation of Vaughan's inhabiting of the Bible, with detailed reference to many of the poems in *Silex II*. But what has been gleaned so far from these brief sketches is ample for combining reflection with action.

To conclude, Thomas Calhoun expresses Vaughan's commitment to this vital way of faith:

> No similitude, idea or edict will change the nature of others or the world. But hope lies in one man's capacity for sustained lament of the human condition that, guided by a vision of original and resurrected life, extends and manifests itself in acts of charity.[48]

---

[48] Calhoun, p. 205.

frogs and lilies
by Ann Lewis

FRANCES-ANNE KING

Balnakeil

Do you remember the exhibition we visited that day –
the microscope laid out for us to look through,

the smear of sand across the slide that changed
under the lens to multicoloured particles of stone,

glass, rock, shell, each with their own identity, and how
despite their journey through millennia battered

and ground by seas, they still survive to illustrate
geology. The mass of soft piled dunes which spill

onto this Scottish beach in woven shades of gold
bear all our weight; we leave our footprints

with those of oyster catchers, black headed gulls
and arctic terns. Whatever we choose to give

to the sand of ourselves it takes and disperses
to the wind's will or the wash of a cleansing tide.

CHARLES WILKINSON

'brumeux'

so no way back to then,
the time of mists, & each
act of remembering fogs
anew
       how the fool dwells
on early mornings, mistakes
dew for gemstones, clean
& cut by unclouded sun.
if warm memory meets
cool past, truth must smaze:
what's been is now forever
hazed by present perception:
the gift of that day's light
a blaze that will smoke out
phantom facts, half seen
&, when found, blurred
by retrieval
       yet dawn, loomed
from night, brings the silks
of brume curling from earth
to cover land from sight
       a sky's
near white lisse conceals the flair
of older weather, a talent for
eternal holiday
       & still a longing
for what might burn through,
so nothing's suspended here,
till all the perfect hours collect,
as one, lifted into timeless blue.

BRUCE MCRAE

The Hive's Heart

At the heart of the hive
is a kitchen warmly lit in midwinter.
There's a voice describing gold and yellow,
their small but many differences.
At the heart of the hive
is a vase containing buttercups.
There's an altar and a candle,
offerings to the god of suns.
Unearthly music can be heard,
an allurement sending bees into madness,
those clever carpenters and wheelwrights,
those busy emissaries with love on their lips.
How brief are their lives, how sweet their desperation.

PETER LIMBRICK

Poet

Ease me out of bed in the morning
Wash all my legs
Set me on the windowsill
Launch me into the air
At dusk when I return
Pull the ribbons from my wings
Dust the music from my scales
Let me sip wine at your feet

It was a short meeting

it was a short meeting
with her father
no time for the usual pleasantries
nor to apologise
for breaking his neck
as she rushed past
to keep her appointment
with the windscreen

THOR BACON

Isölte & Tristan

Please don't say the dull knife is more dangerous.
She blows out a candle; thunder cracks in a valley
as meadowlarks crouch in the rising breeze.

Since Sunday school I've heard it as *I don't want a Shepherd*.
They say Prophet Abraham drew the blade, not once,
but a hundred times over Isaac's unyielding throat.

Let's not talk about the heart just yet, okay?
We notice our leftovers gone in the fridge and grit our teeth.
All we'll find on Mars is the stone club that killed Kennedy.

In Berkeley, a Chinese healer speaks of a man
who came for something to cool his burning knee:
after an hour with a heating pad, he walked out, cured.

This is right about where they'll say *I told you so*,
but that's okay. I am Isölt catching sight of that black sail.
I am Tristan dreaming in the hollow oak.

My only comfort is knowing you followed
these marks trailing over the page-white snow –
and your hands warming this spine as the words trail off.

JOHN WELCH

Gardening

Slow mover, walking up the hill,
A scent of wallflower. April's
A cold-hot cloud-bright Sunday.
In Harrow almost in heaven
A modest light shines on brickwork.
The mode here is mock-Georgian
Blood-red flowers on the rhododendrons
Cotoneaster's dull glimmer
The dried-out beds of last year's leaves
And for those who don't care for gardening
really
There's the modest-institutional mode
In troughs of concrete, soil like dried blood
The peat from defeated moorlands, ghosts of
forests.

Her being alone whole days
Devoted to the destruction of weeds
Grubs hugging their jackets of earth,
Petrified cat shit
Grown inoffensive as soil, remembers
Dried flower arrangements spattered with silver
On the rosewood table's
Ghostly artifice of polish,
But how to disentangle
Imagination from death? She'll discover
Chaired in her hands a ball
Of fibrous matter dumped on the ground.

'The geums need tidying –
Those ones have turned out red'
Delphiniums, sprouting such baby softness of leaf.
Now a hot light sunders the trees.
Those trees over there look bridal
A gauze of leaves going on and on,
Sundays in Harrow, to moulder in heaven.
Moving away down the hill
Were faces screwed up against sunlight,
Soil sown with flint and pebbles
As a breeze came to rest in the conifers.
A plant life is the one we aspire to.
Deeper than feeling the roots creep
Under the paving stones. Recover the surface,
With a small fork worry the soil.
She gardens around a death,
Carries the weeds in gloved hands.

Someone

No the house was not empty
Not totally. There was someone there
Arranging flowers, dusting the tables
Preparing food. There was someone
Leaning over the banisters,
Someone who turned to him, saying
'You do not know me at all'.

Outside some others were waiting
Standing beside their car, their faces
Bright with expectancy. But he went back
To his own face staring out of the mirror, back
To where the clock quartered the sighing hours.

Each day is like this now.
Each morning she brings him
His own head on a dish, staring.

EDMUND MATYJASZEK

A Crocus Field

After the long winter, the crocus found it
Painful to open. Bruised in its sides,
The flushed curve of colour it would spear
For first light of spring
Was pinched, pounded by relentless rain.

Caution ruled. Only a tentative
Hint of sun. Then suddenly, one day,
The air changed; the blue sky spread; an unfamiliar
Mildness. Almost as if
A battle-field had cleared, and dazed and
astonished,
They woke to victory.
                                        Survivors
Out of foxholes, at corners of lawns, battered
Edges of grassland, in thin, impoverished columns
Appeared, stumbling, unsure, watchful
Of inclement skies, of yet more rain.

But with each day, a bolder purple,
A sweet bright white, and their insignia –
That yellow talisman of hope.

CAROL BARBOUR

Althernal Walk

Astride the witness
reflective eye blinks
sun infiltrates the street
eroding grass with the flood
that came last month
and receded just in time.

A star in traction aimed
outward. A shrub of Jericho
glistens with the sprinkle of water.
High and dry, I take care
no matter what comes up
at the radiation lab.

A star burst cluster on the ground.
I pin it on my sweater to indicate
membership in the order
of the vagabonds.
It is not romantic or
bohemian, but rather
apropos for the time being.

LINDA BLACK

Rails of dresses

hem-locked wind-blown
true dress skew dress a scantling
of hope lattice

wear   waisted
unbuttoned gathered
& primed – the colour
of brass worn in a field
side-swept a hand
holding a hat
ribbons flaying

PATRICK BOND

The Bone Room

...*like this, like this* – Rumi, tr C. Barks

after the lights are turned out
and night fills room after room
when screens and radios have calmed down
I sit in the bone room, the charnel house

I do not belong here yet
I come to get to know them
say hello for the first time in years
an elbow, a foot, an eye socket

come to get the feel of the place
space in between, the hollow in the cavities
place of viscera, of a womb
of a heart, breath, brain

I am not here yet, my spaces still full
and hospital trolleys specially shaped
tubes and bags and connections wait
to touch and hold and comfort me

but now I am in the bone room and they sing
of dust beyond dying, honeycombs of wonder
particles and grains of us earth-souled
returning and dispersing, they say, *like this, like this*

SHANTA ACHARYA

Snowy Egret

Smeared in ash, head bent in the morning mist,
one leg crooked, resembling an Indian yogi,

the snowy egret meditates beyond regret
and desire on the struggle to assuage hunger.

Perched on a boulder at the edge of the river
that keeps retreating every season, he waits –

a seasoned fisherman poised for a catch,
for a taste of flesh to freshen his mouth fouled

by plastic. Suddenly, he darts forward, dives in,
scoops a mouthful of quivering slivers.

Standing upright he savours the moment,
rapt in the dazzling company of clouds.

Lifting a creel of sunshine, he spreads his wings
with the grace of a ballet dancer retreating –

unaware of his separateness, one with the light
soaring on his back to the call of the universe.

In Silence

When fate deals you a losing hand, play in silence.
Luck favours those who mend themselves in silence.

Remember precious lessons learnt in defeat –
pearls of experience purchased in silence.

A game of chance, nothing in this world is real,
our stories shadows passing in silence.

Be the flame of a candle to what blows you –
life is the greatest gift bestowed in silence.

Days are restless until your heart finds a home,
a sky where you can be yourself in silence.

Earth's grand gardens may beckon you in your dreams,
love's a patch of green that flowers in silence –

a shade that shelters you in times of crises,
a place you keep returning to in silence.

To hold, be held the Beloved eternal –
believe in the splendour of grace in silence.

Silence is the keeper of keys to secrets –
Shantih that passes understanding in silence.

Note: *Silence is the keeper of keys to secrets* from 'Things' by Agha Shahid Ali, *Call Me Ishmael Tonight* (W.W. Norton & Company, New York/London: 2003). '*Shantih*' in Sanskrit means peace.

NOEL CANIN

Memories and Ashes

I
In the Drakensburg, mist drifts down the air,
dampens the noses of wild mountain ponies,
tails flicking the slanted rain.

II
You used to run through the rain,
wet shine on cheek bones, willing hands
catching mid-air. I remember this.

III
Here on Revivim, mist like powdered steam
falls diagonally to the earth.
Beyond the orchards, beyond the graveyard,
the desert unrolls.

IV
In your home in Johannesburg, your walking stick
hangs on the banister.
The narrow stairs where
Ella rushed to catch you one morning
when the crutches slipped.
I remember you telling me this.

V
Afterwards, the man who said he loved you
carried your ashes into the mountains–
        your spot, the tent, brave
          red dot at the root of the mountain–
released you into a white-pebbled stream–
        I forgave him much for this.

CLARE CROSSMAN

The Territory of Water

(after Coleridge. Kubla Kahn)

On Neptune Street,
you may be dreaming of how the tide
will take you South to where two seas
meet, halfway to Africa, halfway to Spain.
Along the shore the harbour opens;
black sea shingle and the scudding tide.

One bag on your shoulder
clanking with all you possess
like a sailor, you will come to know the ocean
the departure, the arrival, the return.

Once boarded for the journey,
there is no going back, unless the compass
sets a course for home.
The deck will heave and roll
below the flight of cormorants
above the whispering sea.
Where storms break mountainous waves,
and calm is flat and stifling,
the sky a lid that can't be lifted.

In the territory of water
the book of maps you opened,
will fill with fire flies gold ignition.
Sudden changes in weather.
Red burn of sun on sea,
the purple outlines of harbours,
their unknown warmth and scents,
sail bound jetties, beyond grey.

Vermillion dusting your hands,
 in black wet October,
turning pages will tell about
the wind you saw.
The glint at each corner
of the constellations,
the tin cup of water lifted,
the sky inking,
poems, songs and legends.

Sharing in the building:
The Creative Relationship of R.S. Thomas and Elsi Eldridge

Tony Brown

In 1937 a young woman artist named Mildred Elsi Eldridge (known to her family and friends as 'Elsie', later cymricised to 'Elsi') was teaching art at Moreton Hall School, a public school for girls near Chirk. She'd been in the area since 1935, teaching initially at Oswestry High School, living in lodgings with two spinster ladies who ran a shop. This was very much a change of scene for Eldridge: she was from Leatherhead in Surrey, the daughter of a jeweller; she'd gone to Wimbledon School of Art from where, in 1930, she had won a scholarship to the Royal College of Art. In 1933, at the end of her studies at the R.C.A., she had won a travelling scholarship enabling her to travel for some months in 1934 in Italy, sketching and painting; she visited Rome, Florence, Naples, Capri, Assisi (where she studied Giotto's murals) and Venice. In Florence she'd visited Bernard Berenson, the major collector and dealer at his art-filled villa, I Tatti.[1]

At Oswestry High School she had become friendly with an English teacher, Joan Wood; Wood had been a pupil at Moreton Hall, and later went back there to teach. Presumably it was through Joan Wood that Elsi Eldridge got a job at Moreton Hall. Wood also took in boarders at her substantial home in Chirk, Bryn Coed, and the young art teacher became a lodger there.

---

[1] Biographical details in the present paper are from Eldridge's unpublished autobiographical journal, written in the 1980s. The journal is currently being prepared by myself and Rachael Davenhill for publication.

Moreton Hall had a very Anglican ethos. Former pupils speak with feeling about the march in crocodile every Sunday to St. Mary's Church at Chirk. There were also services during the week in the school hall, some of which were held by the curate from St. Mary's. The art teacher met the young curate, and as they walked in the school grounds together it seems that a strong attachment gradually grew up. Indeed the vicar at Chirk spoke later of his curate having been 'besotted' by the young art teacher.[2]

The curate was Rev. R.S. Thomas, freshly ordained after his Latin degree at Bangor and theological training at Llandaff. I was not surprised when I heard that word 'besotted'. Not only was Elsi Eldridge striking in appearance, as contemporary studio photographs show, but must have seemed to the young Welsh curate to have come from another world – as in many ways she did. His main pastime, when free of his clerical duties, was walking in the countryside at Dyffryn Ceiriog; he'd been brought up in Holyhead, gone as far as Bangor to do his degree, and now after only one year in Llandaff, he was back in north Wales. She, on the other hand, was well-travelled; she spoke French, having spent time in France as a teenager, and had lived in artistic circles in London and Italy. She was also much better read than he was, a point we will return to. She wore brightly-coloured clothes, including on some occasions a rather bohemian cloak. While she was based in Chirk, she had a very successful one-woman exhibition at the Beaux Arts Gallery in London in 1937, so successful indeed that she bought in London a large Bentley convertible, which she brought back to Chirk.

At this point R.S. Thomas was already writing poetry. Indeed, he put together, at about this time, a typed collection

---

[2] Personal interview with Rev. Evelyn Davies, June 2017. (Rev. Davies succeeded R.S. Thomas as vicar at St Hywyn's Church, Aberdaron.)

of his poetry, though whether he sent it to a publisher we do not know. Certainly, it never saw the light of day. The collection, which he called *Spindrift: Poems and Prose Poems,* is composed of what we might politely call apprentice pieces, not developed technically from the poems he'd been writing as a student in Bangor. They are almost without exception lyrical evocations of the natural world, suffused with the unfocused romantic longings of the narrating voice, who wanders alone, often at evening or at dusk: '...the mystic hour, / When whitely shone the unknown flower, / And darkling wings had swept away / The last pale streamers of the day [...]' ('Strumblegilfin'); 'After the languor of this idle day [...] / The wild bee hums / No more, yet memory of his song / Still lingers in the gray gnats' silken wings'... ('Evening'). Almost inevitably, such lyrical sentiment occasionally topples into sentimentality: 'Beauty was born when a little wave / Lost himself in a dark sea cave, / And there in the silence his cries awoke / The voices of the numerous long-lost folk' ('Beauty'). It is hard to believe that this young versifying curate was to become a major poet. It is all pretty poor stuff, indebted to the languid melancholy of the *fin-de-siecle* and to the bookish ruralism of the lesser Georgian poets, with the occasional echo of Keats ('But yester eve I found a maid at rest / Beside a half reaped field of corn reclined', 'Sonnet'). The register is consistently dated ('Behold', 'cometh', 'thou art'); there is no sign of Thomas being at all aware of Modernists like Yeats or Eliot, let alone the contemporary W.H. Auden. [3]

But then there is this, entitled just 'Sonnet':

I never thought in this poor world to find

---

[3] A copy of *Spindrift* is in the archive of the R.S. Thomas Research Centre, Bangor University (hereafter RSTRC). All poems are quoted by permission of R.S. Thomas's estate. © Elodie Thomas.

> Another who had loved the things I love,
> The wind, the trees, the cloud-swept sky above;
> One who was beautiful and grave and kind,
> Who struck no discord in my dreaming mind,
> Content to live with silence as a cloak
> About her every thought, or, if she spoke,
> Her gentle voice was music on the wind.
> And then about the ending of a day
> In early Spring, when the soft western breezes
> Had chased the melancholy clouds afar,
> As up a little hill I took my way,
> I found you all alone upon your knees,
> Your face uplifted to the evening star.[4]

Again, the setting is rural and the time is dusk. But unlike the other vague, almost diaphanous rural 'maids' who do occasionally appear in *Spindrift*, here, however sketchily, the woman is characterised and there is some sense of a relationship between her and the narrator, a relationship of shared interests and attitudes. We note that the woman is 'Content to live with silence as a cloak'; we register that cloak, reminiscent of the one which Eldridge frequently wore (the silence we'll come back to). For I think it highly likely that this was the young R.S. Thomas's first poem to the woman who was to become his wife. In *Neb*, his Welsh-language autobiography (*Neb*: Nobody or Anybody), Thomas writes rather vaguely that Elsi Eldridge was 'lodging fairly close by'.[5] In fact he is being a bit discreet here: by the time they were married, in Bala in 1940,

---

[4] The poem was first collected in R.S. Thomas, *Uncollected Poems*, ed. Tony Brown and Jason Walford Davies (Tarset: Bloodaxe, 2013), p. 22.
[5] R.S. Thomas, *Autobiographies*, trans. Jason Walford Davies (London: Dent, 1997), p. 43.

Sharing in the building'

he also lived at Bryn Coed, in a room along a landing from hers. After marriage they moved to Tallarn Green, near Wrexham, where he became curate, and then, in 1942, to Manafon, near Newtown, Montgomeryshire, where he published his first collection *The Stones of the Field* in 1946.[6] This was a book which collected the poems which he had been publishing in magazines in Wales and Ireland since 1940. His wife drew the cover illustration.

What is remarkable is the difference between *these* poems and the emotion-washed, unfocused verses in *Spindrift*. The major influence in this change, this imaginative focusing, is the presence of Elsi Eldridge. She plays, I think, a crucial role at this point in making R.S. Thomas a poet. In a later poem called 'Careers' (published in 1968) in which the poet reviews his life to date, Thomas writes: 'I am one now / with another. Before I had time / to complete myself, I let her share / in the building. This that I am now [...]'.[7] Indeed, the very fact of her being an artist, and a successful one, seems to have confirmed Thomas in his own determination to succeed as a poet; he writes in *Neb* (where he writes of himself throughout in the third person), 'She had already exhibited her work in galleries in London, and he too yearned to prove himself in his field'.[8] There is no point in speculating as to quite how R.S. Thomas's work would have developed stylistically and how his career as a poet would have evolved without Elsi Eldridge, but it is evident that, from the outset and through the fifty years of their marriage, though their medium of expression was different and they certainly each maintained the integrity of their own artistic activity,

---

[6] The collection was published by Keidrych Rhys's Druid Press, based in Carmarthen.
[7] R.S. Thomas, *Collected Poems 1945-1990* (London: Dent, 1993), p. 181. Further references to *Collected Poems* will be included in the text (*CP*).
[8] *Autobiographies*, p. 45.

interests and attitudes were shared and mutually reinforced, as we shall see.

But how *exactly* did the young artist whom Thomas married affect him in these earliest years? Here are the unpublished recollections of Denise Bates, whom Elsi Eldridge had taught at Moreton Hall and who herself became a professional artist:

> She was small, slender, graceful – quick movements, quick smile, a long stride [...] She wore soft colours– greeny blues, circular swirling skirts [...] She introduced us to contemporary work – [it was] wartime and we couldn't travel much – but we saw a mixed show (in Shrewsbury?) – Graham Sutherland's thorn bushes – landscape details – and she showed – and lent us – books. Stanley Spencer. Her ENTHUSIASM – 'Look, *look*' [...] You know her murals – her observation, use of pattern, plants, bracken, birds, slate fences, lichen, Welsh hills [...] She taught us to look and use what we saw – and to marvel at God's natural world.[9]

We notice how up-to-date Eldridge was and Denise Bates also mentions her drawing her pupils' attention to the work of Laura Knight. Eldridge was aware, too, of modern poetry in a way that R.S. Thomas certainly was not at this point. She writes in 1940 to another pupil, Dorothy Buckland, who was about to go off to study at what was then the University College of Wales, Aberystwyth: 'Never stop reading poetry and try to live it all your life. There has been no man more truly a poet than Yeats, as you know – he is the most completely poetic person I

---

[9] Unpublished notes prepared in 2004. Copy at RSTRC. I am grateful to Denise Bates' daughter, Alison Rylands, for permission to quote this passage.

Sharing in the building'

know'.[10] She was no doubt saying the same to her husband; certainly he seems to be reading Yeats by this time; indeed, he had given Elsi a new collection of Yeats's plays in 1939.[11] But let us return to Denise Bates' recollection of Elsi urging the girls to 'Look'. This was part of her own training at the Royal College of Art, of course, where detailed drawing was a key part of the course. That intense *looking* and precise draughtsmanship was a feature of her own work throughout her career, especially her detailed studies of birds and natural life. In old age she writes in her journal: 'Most people only glance at things [...] The sensitive exploration of colour takes a lifetime of detailed looking'.

By the time of R.S. Thomas's first published poems, the pallid, literary-derived natural scenes of the *Spindrift* poems are replaced by an altogether more precise *looking* at the world itself; Thomas had evidently been listening to his wife, and indeed looking at her pictures too:

> And, bare as a sky, the wind-sucked bone shows blue;
> And berried blood swells in the frosted vein... [12]

In 'The Airy Tomb' (1946), Twm, the farm boy, has seen

> [...] a hawk floating in a bubbling pool,
> Its weedy entrails mocking the breast
> Laced with bright water...   (*CP* 18)

And in 'Farm Child' (1946) the reader is urged to

---

[10] Unpublished letter from from Elsi Eldridge to Dorothy Buckland, 24 September 1940. Copy at RSTRC.
[11] The inscribed copy is in the collection of Thomas's books at RSTRC
[12] 'The Strange Spring', *The Stones of the Field*, p. 26. The poem was first published in 1944.

> Mark how the sun has freckled his smooth face
> Like a finch's egg under that bush of hair
> That dares the wind. (*CP* 41)

It seems unlikely to be wholly a coincidence that in one of Eldridge's notebooks from this time we find a number of pages of exquisitely-drawn and very detailed water-colour sketches of speckled birds' eggs of varying species. R.S. Thomas and Elsi Eldridge's son, Gwydion Thomas, commented in an interview that he thought that 'When RS met Elsi he was visually illiterate. Elsi opened his eyes to detail and colour, to shape and form'.[13] In fact one might go further and argue that it is not merely a matter of the language and imagery of the poems but of the *stance* which the poet takes towards the world in the poetry of the 1940s and 1950s that is relevant here. The early poems are in many ways a record of the young priest seeking to understand the parish in rural Montgomeryshire into which he had been sent, seeking to come to terms with the unfamiliar way of life he found there. Thus the narrator in the early published poems is an intent *looker* at the rural world around him and at the farming people who inhabited it, the people who were Thomas's parishioners. The act of *looking*, usually from a distance, with the narrator as intermediary between reader and the rural community, becomes a recurring motif: in 'The Mistress', for example, the reader is urged to consider the plight of the farm labourer: 'See how earth claims him as he passes by' (*CP* 9); in 'The Welsh Hill Country' it is 'Too far for you to see / The fluke and the foot-rot and the fat maggot / Gnawing the skin from the small bones, [...] / Too far for you to see / The moss and the mould on the cold chimneys' (*CP* 22). The reader

---

[13] '"Quietly as Snow": Gwydion Thomas interviewed by Walford Davies', *New Welsh Review*, No. 64 (Summer 2004), p. 45.

Sharing in the building'

cannot see, but the poet himself has observed and noted. In what is probably Thomas's best-known poem, 'A Peasant', as Iago Prytherch rests by his fire at the end of the day, we are asked to 'see him fixed in his chair' (*CP* 4) while in 'Enigma', 'A man is in the fields. Let us look with his eyes'.[14] Elsewhere in these early poems the poet urges the reader to 'Study this man [...] / Look at his eyes, that are colourless as rain' ('Man and Tree', *CP* 7) and to 'Consider this man in the field beneath' ('Affinity', *CP* 8).

And while RS was learning to look at the countryside around them and to write about it, his wife was looking at him. Unsurprisingly perhaps, Elsi Eldridge drew her husband throughout their marriage; the pictures (of which what follows is a selection, reproduced here in black and white) become a moving record of their fifty years together. There are, perhaps unsurprisingly, more drawings from these early years than from other periods of their life together. Of the two which we have from 1940, the year of their marriage, one is especially romantic, showing Thomas with a mop of curly hair, a somewhat fanciful image of a young poet (fig.1); the other, to judge from contemporary photographs, is a somewhat more realistic image, albeit drawn in a red pencil, echoing the Renaissance portraits which she had seen in Italy (fig. 2). A drawing from 1944 rather unexpectedly shows Thomas with a beard; Gwydion Thomas related the story that when Thomas arrived on a visit to his parents' house in Holyhead, his formidable mother urged him to shave it off, which he evidently did (fig.3). A tender drawing of R.S. Thomas sleeping was done in the 1940s, when the couple were at Manafon (fig. 4). Eldridge tells the story in her autobiographical journal that when she sent the picture ('rather a good study', in her view) to

---

[14] R.S. *Thomas, An Acre of Land* (Newtown: Montgomeryshire Printing Co., 1952), p. 31.

the Royal Watercolour Society for exhibition, 'It was sent back to me with a note to say "We are not in the habit of exhibiting studies of dead men"'.[15] A later drawing (fig. 5), done in 1978, is an evocation of a manifestly older R.S. Thomas, though the strong bone structure and wild curly hair gives the portrait considerable power. The drawing was used as the frontispiece of Moelwyn Merchant's 1979 study of Thomas in the influential 'Writers of Wales' series and this possibly suggests some sort of approval of the image by its subject.[16] A drawing done the previous year (fig. 6) exists, as far as I know, only in a photograph, taken by Eldridge.[17] It is evidently a *study* not a final picture–she is looking intently: we notice the carefully-drawn details of his mouth and his lobe-less ears in the margins of the picture. It is rather reminiscent of some of her bird studies where she gives details alongside the main picture of individual feathers or of the head or wing. We don't know if the picture was ever actually completed. In my view this is the most powerful and moving of all of Eldridge's portraits of her husband. It seems to go beneath the surface to hint at some inner stress. In fact this is the year before Thomas retired from the Church, the prelude to the years of frequently anguished spiritual reflection which we see in those magnificent religious poems of the 1980s. One final portrait by Elsi Eldridge (fig. 7)

---

[15] The image of the scarecrow in the background recurs in Eldridge's work at this time, including the illustrations she did for Faber's new edition of Henry Williamson's *The Star-Born* (London: Faber, 1948), p.105 and the illustrations facing pp. 118 and 186. The cruciform scarecrow is frequently suggestive of the Crucifixion.

[16] Moelwyn Merchant, *R.S. Thomas* (Cardiff: U. of Wales P., 1979). In fact, given the dates of book and drawing, it is possible that the portrait was especially commissioned.

[17] The photograph is in the collection of the RSTRC, as are figures 1, 3 and 7. Figure 5 is in the collection of the National Portrait Gallery. The other two pictures are in private collections. All pictures © The Estate of M.E. Eldridge.

Sharing in the building'

came to light only in 2017 in a major sale of her work held in London.[18] It is a powerful image, in pencil with white gouache, drawn in 1981 at the small cottage at Sarn y Plas, near Aberdaron at the far tip of the Lleyn Peninsula, where the couple lived after Thomas's retirement from the Church in Wales in 1978. Again we have the strong bone structure and the wild hair, highlighted by the gouache. Thomas is wearing the fisherman's smock in which he walked the hills and shores

(figure 1)

---

[18] The sale was by Abbott and Holder at their gallery in Bloomsbury. See http://www.abbottandholder-thelist.co.uk/mildred-eldridge-exhibition-2017/
The portrait of R.S. Thomas was purchased by the R.S. Thomas Research Centre, with financial support from the University's Development Fund, and is exhibited in a public area at Bangor University.

of the area at this time.[19]

(figure 2)

---

[19] The portrait is drawn on a sheet of paper taped to a piece of board, though the image, especially the hair, bursts beyond the paper onto the tape and board. On the verso of the board is a landscape painting by Eldridge, evidently dating from her time in Italy in 1934.

Sharing in the building'

(figure 3)

(figure 4)

(figure 5)

(figure 6)

Sharing in the building'

(figure 7)

But let us go back again to 1938-9 and consider another picture by Elsi Eldridge that only exists in a photograph taken by her (fig. 8).[20] It is a picture of a mural which she painted, in about 1938, for the Ibis Club, in Chiswick, which was a social club for employees of the Prudential Insurance Company. The building is still there – it is now a private sports club – but the painting seems no longer to exist. But it is a fascinating early image of Eldridge's socio-political vision. On the verso of the photograph she has written the title 'The Exploitation of the

[20] The photograph is held by the RSTRC. Another copy is in the archives of the Tate Gallery; it appeared in an exhibition of photos of contemporary murals held at the Tate in 1939. See Eric Newton, 'Mural Paintings', *Sunday Times*, 28 May 1939, p.4, in which Newton refers to the photograph of Eldridge's mural.

Countryside'. The scene is a rural one; in the foreground the corn is ripe and ready for harvest. But unlike other Eldridge paintings in the 1930s, where we see groups of female figures in harmony with their rural environment, bringing in the harvest or gathering fruit or indeed playing musical instruments, the figures here appear to be intrusive. Their clothing is rather stylish; these are not country people. The female figure to the left of the centre, with her shadowed eyes, a figure of whom Eldridge made several sketches, seems especially foreboding. And beyond this central group we see the serried ranks of cars, which presumably have brought these people into the countryside. The 1930s was of course the period of the massive expansion of private car ownership and, thus, the building of the A roads in the UK. (The situation necessitated the Road Traffic Act of 1934 which introduced a speed limit for cars of 30 mph in built-up areas.) So this is very much an allusion to the increasingly mechanised contemporary world, a world of speed not rural tranquillity. In the background, on the horizon, we see the smoking chimney stacks, symbols of the industrial urban world. And we notice too the parachutes. This is the late 1930s, the era not only of planes, but of aerial warfare. The Spanish Civil War had been going on since 1936, with air combat and of course bombing. (Eldridge had, we remember, visited Mussolini's Italy: she comments in a letter to her parents that she had seen armed blackshirted Fascists in Rome.[21]) It is a new note in Eldridge's work, a vision of a modern world that is increasingly mechanised; a world in which humanity is in danger of losing its natural roots.

---

[21] Letter from Rome to Mr. and Mrs. F.C. Eldridge, undated [c. 24 March 1934], RSTRC.

Sharing in the building'

(figure 8)

This is an opposition which some dozen or more years later was to find expression in the centrepiece of Elsi's artistic career, the mural which she painted in the early 1950s for the Robert Jones and Agnes Hunt Orthopaedic and Hospital at Gobowen, a vast work, six canvases totalling some 100 feet in width.[22] The mural, which is entitled *The Dance of Life,* again sets up an opposition between a rural world, the world of animals and birds and plants, in which peasant communities live in harmony with each other and with nature, and a world in which human beings have become alienated, lost their roots. The first panel (fig 9), some 20 feet in width, shows a rural scene, in which amongst trees and corn sheaves, a group of female figures in

---

[22] The mural is not painted directly onto the walls but onto a series of six canvas panels, which were then fastened to the walls. The canvases were painted at Eglwysfach and Manafon. The work was commissioned in June 1951 and completed in early 1956.

peasant dress play musical instruments while others dance.[23] In the foreground is a row of bee hives, another symbol of natural community, which features in several of Eldridge's paintings in

(figure 9)

the 1930s. To the far right of the panel a figure is blessing the crops, a ritual which Elsi Eldridge had seen and sketched in Italy. Evidently the costumes were those of a group of Yugoslavian peasant dancers who had appeared at the Llangollen International Eisteddfod and of whose colourful costumes they had allowed Eldridge to make studies, though she had also drawn and painted similar female peasant figures in the fields in her visit to Italy in 1934. The buildings in the far background also suggest Italy, but ultimately the scene in the panel is timeless and unlocated, emblematising, as the notes

---

[23] The central figure, playing a bagpipe appears to be a self portrait of the artist. She is the only figure in the whole mural who looks directly out of the frame at the viewer. Eldridge had seen traditional peasant bagpipes in Italy and indeed brought home with her a postcard showing bagpipe players.

Sharing in the building'

which Eldridge supplied to the hospital explained, humanity 'in complete harmony with nature'.[24]

After a series of smaller panels showing a series of rural scenes, the birds and animals painted with Eldridge's usual detailed observation, the fifth panel, some fourteen feet in width, provides a stark contrast to the first (fig.10). To the left a naked couple, 'emanations of the first man and woman', appear in anguished postures among trees which are stark and leafless. When viewed closely, it is evident that the woman's hand and foot which are visible bear the stigmata while at her left foot there is a snake: this is manifestly a fallen world. To the right of the panel are 'a group of three figures who seek pleasure in making music, not with the complete freedom of enjoyment as the three peasants in panel 1, but with the knowledge of death lurking in the veil of life, which surrounds them'. Indeed, amongst the Spencer-like veils there is a skeleton. This part of the scene is set in a modern urban world ('the monotonous row of houses suggests the monotony of life that man has made for himself in the towns'), with sheets of newspapers descending on the people in the background. To the extreme right a single figure flees from the 'manmade city' to an open, natural seascape.

---

[24] The notes were in fact written by Louis Behrend, who with his wife Mary were major patrons of the arts; they commissioned Stanley Spencer to paint the Sandham Memorial chapel at Burghclere in memory of Mary Behrend's brother, who died at the end of the First World War. They came to live at Llanwrin, near Egwysfach, and became close friends with Elsi Eldridge. One assumes that the notes on the mural were written in consultation with her; when Alan Powers used the notes in an essay on the mural, Eldridges wrote approvingly in her journal, describing them as 'accurate and sane'. Further quotations regarding the mural are from these notes. See Alan Powers, 'Wards and Walls', *Country Life*, 17 March 1988, pp. 96-7. The Behrends took Spencer to see the mural and he sent Eldridge a lengthy and enthusiastic letter of appreciation (14 November 1958).

(figure 10)

In the final panel 'Man seeks to preserve his life by inventing machines'. In the background, as in 'The Exploitation of the Countryside', chimneys belch smoke, while elsewhere the parachutes recur along with jet fighters whose insignia suggests American fighters in the Korean War which was being waged as Eldridge painted her work. In the foreground (fig.11) 'children play in a world of their own, oblivious of man and his machines': the children play with animals and birds, responding innocently and imaginatively to the world that the activities of the adults is threatening to destroy.[25]

---

[25] The mural is now to be seen in the foyer of the Centre for the Creative Industries at Glyndwr University, Wrexham. Pictures of the mural during the process of conservation can be seen at: https://www.flickr.com/photos/glyndwruniversity/albums/72157625399291630

Sharing in the building'

If we consider for a moment the themes we find in R.S. Thomas's poetry of this period in the 1950s, we can see at once how closely allied is his vision to that which we see in his wife's work. I would argue that the central tension in R.S. Thomas's work is that between, on the one hand, a life which is rural, simple, quiet, a place where the imagination can thrive, the imagination which, for Thomas, gives access to the spiritual.[26] 'The Moor' was written in the 1950s, when he was in Eglwysfach:

(figure 11)

---

[26] I am using 'imagination' in the sense that the Romantic poets used it, as Thomas was well aware. In the Introduction to his *Penguin Book of Religious Verse,* for instance, Thomas refers to Coleridge in his *Biographia Literaria,* where the operation of the human imagination is the 'repetition in the finite mind of the Infinite I AM'. Thus, 'The nearest we approach to God, he appears to say, is as creative beings'. The poet through his work brings the imagination of the reader into activity, sensitises the imaginative capacity of the individual, and this brings him/her 'nearer to the primary imagination [...] nearer to the actual being of God' (R.S. Thomas, *Selected Prose,* ed. Sandra Anstey (Bridgend: Seren, 2nd ed. 1995), p. 48.) For Thomas, as for the Romantics, especially Wordworth, the imaginative capacities were most likely to be stimulated into activity by the natural world.

It was like a church to me.
I entered it on soft foot,
Breath held like a cap in the hand.
It was quiet.
What God was there made himself felt,
Not listened to, in clean colours
That brought a moistening of the eye,
In movement of the wind over grass. [...]

I walked on,
Simple and poor, while the air crumbled
And broke on me generously as bread. (*CP* 166)

On the other hand, in direct contrast to this rural world of the imaginative vitality and spiritual awareness, is the modern urban world, the world of mass production and mass consumerism, the world of the Machine, which is embodied as a sort of threatening cartoon character in Thomas's collection *H'm* (1972).[27] The world of the Machine, and of machine thinking, is a world from which the imagination and the spiritual have disappeared. It is a vision that is present in his poetry as early as 'Cynddylan on a Tractor' (first published in *An Acre of Land*), where Thomas's Welsh rural worker is now proudly mechanised:

Gone the old look that yoked him to the soil;
He's a new man now, part of the machine,
His nerves of metal and his blood oil [...]

He is the knight at arms breaking the fields'
Mirror of silence, emptying the wood

---

[27] R.S. Thomas, *H'm* (London: Macmillan, 1972).

Sharing in the building'

> Of foxes and squirrels and bright jays.
> The sun comes over the tall trees
> Kindling all the hedges, but not for him
> Who runs his engine on a different fuel (*CP* 30)

Cynddylan may no longer be yoked to the soil, but the price he plays for his new mobility is that of being cut off from the natural world, isolated in an imaginatively impoverished world. The poem was published in 1952. Elsi Eldridge was painting her mural.

We recall the reference in the commentary notes to the 'monotonous row of houses', suggesting 'the monotony of life that man has made for himself in the towns' in the mural; in R.S. Thomas's 'Abercuawg', an important address given at the National Eisteddfod in 1976, the mythical, idealised Abercuawg, a sun-filled place of 'trees and fields and flowers and bright unpolluted streams', essentially a transfigured Wales, is contrasted with the modern urban world's

> [...] endless streets of modern, characterless
> houses, each with its garage and television
> aerial, a place from where the trees and the
> birds and the flowers have fled before the yearly
> extension of concrete and tarmacadam; where
> the people do the same kind of soul-less,
> monotonous work to provide for still more and
> more of their kind.[28]

This is, for Thomas, the nightmarish world of the machine, our modern world where the individual is merely a function of mass production and mass consumption:

---

[28] *Selected Prose*, p. 125.

The tins marched to the music
Of the conveyer belt. A billion
Mouths opened. Production,
Production, the wheels

Whistled. Among the forests
Of metal the one human
Sound was the lament of
The poets for deciduous language.
('Postscript', CP 225)

Thus in so many ways, although working in different media, R.S. Thomas and Elsi Eldridge's outlook on the world seems to be strikingly in accord. In fact, given what we see of Eldridge's vision in that mural 'The Exploitation of the Countryside', which dates from about 1938, when she and her future husband would have known each other for only a very short time, one might speculate that her influence on his developing ideas might have been as potent as her effect on his verse style, or at very least that they were two young people with sympathetic ideas about the world which were mutually developed as their relationship grew. In one of his autobiographical essays, for instance, Thomas comments that, at Chirk, 'My painter friend, Elsi [...] shared my inner dissatisfaction with modern society. We dreamed of breaking away, and going to live in a cottage "on water and a crust"'.[29] In the event they did not 'break

---

[29] R.S. Thomas, 'Autobiographical Essay' in *Miraculous Simplicity: Essays on R.S. Thomas*, ed. William V. Davis (Fayetteville: U. of Arkansas P., 1993), p. 6. Thomas is recalling Keats' reference in 'Lamia' to 'Love in a hut, with water and a crust'. (This twenty-page essay, first published in the U.S.A. in 1986, differs in some respects from his Welsh-language accounts of his life, 'Y Llwybrau Gynt' (1972) and *Neb* (1985), both translated in *Autobiographies*.)

Sharing in the building'

away' and drop out of their society, though they did go off together camping in the north Wales countryside as well as venturing, in the little Austin 7 which replaced Eldridge's Bentley convertible, to the Scottish isles and to rural Ireland. At the same time it is worth underlining that Eldridge's vision of the rural-urban polarity does not take on the nationalist perspective that Thomas's does.

*

We have seen Elsi Eldridge's portraits of her husband, how *she* looked at *him*. What of R.S. Thomas's view of her and indeed of their complex, and creative, fifty-year relationship? His first reference to his wife in a published poem would seem to be in 'Ap Huw's Testament' (1958) where she appears amongst 'the four people in my life, / Father, mother, wife / And the one child':

> Let me begin
> With her of the immaculate brow
> My wife; she loves me. I know how.
> (CP 83)

It could scarcely be more restrained. Indeed, I'd argue that that final line is moving *because* of the restraint. He knows how, but he will not, or perhaps is unable to, express it to the reader. This restraint is typical of many of the poems to his wife in her lifetime. Asked by a journalist, after her death, if he had 'loved Elsi deeply', Thomas answered with rather painful honesty: 'I don't think I am a very loving person [...]. I wasn't brought up in a loving home – my mother was afraid of emotion and you tend to carry on in the same way, don't you?'[30] In a remarkable moment in an interview with Byron Rogers, R.S. Thomas's biographer, Gwydion Thomas commented on his father's 'rather dour exterior, as people thought, and rather unfriendly and rather unloving and possibly acerbic, I mean inside he was obviously seething, seething with love and seething with emotion'.[31] Gwydion Thomas said to me on one occasion that he felt his father was 'all bottled up' emotionally.

Clearly such a temperament is going to result in a relationship which is perhaps not going to be easy and open and certainly not effusive and, again, this is reflected in the poetry. 'Anniversary' is, once more, despite the occasion, marked by its reticence; there is no first-person 'I', just one 'we' and one 'us': here's the first stanza:

> Nineteen years now
> Under the same roof
> Eating our bread,
> Using the same air;
> Sighing, if one sighs,
> Meeting the other's
> Words with a look
> That thaws suspicion. (*CP* 103)

Those participles, which continue through the poem, seem to me to express the continuing *process* – negotiation, interaction – which is the essence of this marriage, a process in which they

---

[30] Graham Turner, 'God is a poet who sang creation', *Daily Telegraph*, 4 December 1999, Arts Section, p. 1ff.
[31] Gwydion Thomas, Interview with Byron Rogers, p. 41. I am quoting from a transcription of an uncut version of the interview which formed part of *On Show: R.S. Thomas: The Man Who Went into the West*, BBC2 Wales, 25 November 2006. The video and typed transcription of the interview are at the RSTRC.

Sharing in the building'

are both involved; there's no active 'I' or 'you'. 'Under the same roof' doesn't necessarily express intimacy and the possibility of 'suspicion' as a source of unease in a relationship is openly registered. But because of the honesty of that recognition, the mutual looking, the mutual *regard* (in both senses), the sharing, is all the more convincing:

> Nineteen years now
> Sharing life's table,
> And not to be first
> To call the meal long
> We balance it thoughtfully
> On the tip of the tongue,
> Careful to maintain
> The strict palate.

The relationship is not only a delicate communion but one of mutual 'care' and respect for the other as a separate individual, a relationship of tact and balance.

They each, through the years, got on with their own lives and work; she with her drawing and painting, he with his writing and, of course, his role as a priest. In each of the houses in which they lived, from the substantial rectory at Manafon to the small cottage at Rhiw, it seems that each had their own area, their own creative space: her studio, his study. Gwydion recalled:

> He'd be at one bit of the house and she'd be in another. [...] They just got on with their lives. Met for meals.[32]

---

[32] Gwydion Thomas, Interview with Byron Rogers, p. 28. This coming together at mealtimes manifestly echoes the images of communion 'Anniversary': 'eating our bread [...] sharing life's table'.

It is a routine, as we have seen, repeatedly registered in the poetry.

Elsi Eldridge was also an avid and expert gardener, creating gardens in each of the houses in which they lived, especially at Aberdaron and in the cottage at Sarn; one journal is largely a diary of her plantings, the progression of flowers and fruit in the face of the weather, and letters to several of her friends indicate her exchanging plants with them. This aspect of her creative life features in a number of the poems which Thomas wrote about her. In the deeply moving 'Together', written after her death in 1991, the poet recalls

> Coming in from the fields
> With my offering of flowers
> I found her garden
> Had forestalled me in providing
> Civilities for my desk.[33]

In 'Dying' – which was not published until after Thomas's death – it is in her garden that he recalls her, even in her final days:

> She does not inflict
> her suffering on the garden,
> but is as a shadow
> disclosing light is about.

---

[33] R.S. Thomas, *Collected Later Poems 1988-2000* (Tarset: Bloodaxe, 2004), p. 315.

Sharing in the building'

> In a corner, offering
> Herself to the sun's healing,
> I found her and discoursed
> Upon everything but death.[34]

After her death, the poet sees the garden 'as / an extension of herself, / as though illness could have a perfume / of its own'. In a much earlier poem simply called 'The Garden' and dating from the Manafon years, the garden is seen as 'a gesture against the wild, / The ungovernable sea of grass; / A place to remember love in [...]' (*CP* 132). That same opposition, between the carefully-tended garden and the wild moorland beyond it, is present in an important poem from the same period entitled 'The Untamed':

> My garden is the wild
>   Sea of the grass. Her garden
> Shelters between walls.
>   The tide could break in;
>   I should be sorry for this. [...]
>
>   Her care
> For green life has enabled
> The weak things to grow.
>
> Despite my first love,
>   I take sometimes her hand,
> Following strait paths
>   Between flowers, the nostril
>   Clogged with their thick scent.   (*CP* 140)

---

[34] R.S. Thomas, *Poems to Elsi*, ed. Damian Walford Davies (Bridgend: Seren, 2013), p. 59. The manuscript of 'Dying' is in the collection of the RSTRC.

Again there remains that sense of each of them having their own areas of activity: he the walker in the wild natural world up on the moors, his 'first love'; she the nurturer of the garden, the civilised space. And we notice that play on 'strait' (constraining, not 'straight' as in a straight line): there is still an anxiety in these poems at times of male selfhood being threatened or constrained by the female that we see elsewhere in Thomas's writing.[35]

'He and She' clearly echoes the domestic routines we have seen in 'Anniversary':

> When he came in, she was there.
> When she looked at him,
> he smiled. There were lights
> in time's wave breaking
> on an eternal shore. (*CP* 459)

Again there is the balance between two selves, echoed in the syntax of the opening lines. Here the silent mutual looking gives rise to an image that is startling in its sudden, and beautiful, widening of perspective. Not for the last time in these poems to Elsi, love is asserted against the inevitable erosion of time's passing. And the mealtime communion here is again silent in its expression:

> Seated at table–
> no need for the fracture
> of the room's silence: noiselessly
> they conversed.

---

[35] See Tony Brown, '"Eve's Ruse": Identity and Gender in the Poetry of R.S. Thomas', *English*, Vol. 49, No. 195 (Autumn 2000), pp. 229-250.

Sharing in the building'

Neither of them, I think, was afraid of silence (indeed for RS in more than one of his religious poems, as he waits in silence for an intuition of God, 'garrulous' is a pejorative). Silence here between the poet and his wife is not born of having nothing to say but of a lack of *necessity* for speech.

R.S. Thomas makes few references in his poems to his wife's art, although it was, manifestly, such a presence in their life together.[36] One of these, 'The Way of It' touchingly sees their marriage as an ongoing part of her creative life:

> With her fingers she turns paint
> into flowers, with her body
> flowers into a remembrance
> of herself. She is at work
> always, mending the garment
> of our marriage [...]
>
>   If there are thorns
> In my life, it is she who
> Will press her breast to them and sing.
>
>   (*CP* 323)

---

[36] Thomas did, unsurprisingly, have a considerable, albeit non-specialist, knowledge of art history. He wrote occasional ekphrastic poems throughout his career. See the Introduction to R.S. Thomas, *Too Brave to Dream: Encounters with Modern Art*, ed. Tony Brown and Jason Walford Davies (Hexham: Bloodaxe, 2016), which also refers (p.13) to the card games which the family played using the 'shoeboxes filled with postcard reproductions of paintings from the Etruscan to the present' which Elsi Eldridge used in her art classes. See also Tony Brown, 'Journey Without Maps: R.S. Thomas's Unpublished Ekphrastic Poems', *Scintilla* 17 (2013), pp. 63-81.

Again, there is no sentimentality: the tensions in a long relationship, the way that a relationship is a process which has to be worked at, is firmly registered in the poem. At the same time her care for him is expressed in terms not only of her painting but of the birds which played such a role in both their lives, in her exquisite paintings and Thomas's birdwatching as well as his poetry. The poems which R.S. Thomas wrote after his wife's death in 1991 are some of his finest; indeed, for me, they are comparable to Thomas Hardy's wonderful elegies to his wife written in 1912-13. 'In Memoriam: MEE', contains one of Thomas's most direct references to Elsi Eldridge's art. The poet is at her grave and he recalls the precision of her studies of nature's fragile beauty, the intensity of her looking ('She explored / all of the spectrum / in a fly's wing') and the poet in turn reconciles the very processes of time with the timeless creativity of her art:

> Others
> will come to this stone
> where, so timeless
> the lichen, so delicate
> its brush strokes,
> it will be as though
> with all windows wide
> in her ashen studio
> she is at work for ever. [37]

Reflecting on his parents' marriage, Gwydion Thomas commented:

---

[37] *Collected Later Poems 1988-2000*, p. 313.

Sharing in the building'

[T]hey had such an extraordinary marriage. [...] They were extremely happy, yes. In the way that people have an extraordinary ability to sense in the significant person the things that will be important and keep them going. They had a lot of shared interests, which I am sure is critical. [38]

Shared interests and, as we have seen, shared views. And one notices that repeated adjective: this was a marriage 'extraordinary' not only in its depth of feeling but, as we have seen, in the nature of its day-to-day routines: this was a shared life of remarkable emotional and creative intensity. Amongst the manuscripts which the Centre at Bangor has purchased in recent years is one more poem by R.S. Thomas to his wife, probably written in her last illness. There are two drafts and the poem may not be finished, but it seems to me to be a moving and effective poem even in this form. It has not previously been published:

> What can I say? I take
> your hand[,] leading you out
> onto the moss-grown
> floor to dance your age's
>
> faltering pavane. Let stiffness
> be grace. Through the eyes'
> window I see a garden
> we have not left, but grown old

---

[38] Interview with Byron Rogers, pp. 23, 26.

SCINTILLA 23

in tending. There is a flower
there that has shed its petals
not annually but day
by day to rebuild itself

on its own ruins.

Syrthiais o dan dy hyd
by Anne Lewis

CLAIRE CROWTHER

The Physics of Coincidence

Like any photon-electron happening
    that makes power,
coincidence carries the angel between.
    Two atoms share

an electron and bond into one body
    in this compass-
ion of matter swaying coincidence
    direct, direct-

ionless as the atoms that keep us, so time
    can herd its lengths
into surprises that rope and skip each to each,
    spiders weaving.

    The hedge of red
swings its fuchsia bells towards your foot falling
    towards my step.
Your arm wings out to a parked car. My curls
               swing.

    Weaving spiders
us through coincidence. Resonates, not does.
    Not one second
that does not resonate coincidence through us.

Confusional in a Gothic Church

*Monsters were staring
and feared for their ends.*

Monsters were staring
from the pews, winged heads

were open-mouthed,
saints modelled cringe

watching souls bare back-
stories in the con-

fessional. They all
stalked god's ad-

vent here, knell-bent. My
lines knelt in couples

and feared for their ends.

NEIL CURRY

Sinai

Month after long winter month of numbing cold,
Then sandstorms, followed by a summer's heat
Such that one brush against a bare rock
Is enough to blister bare flesh; and never
A drop of rain, though snow lingers on
Up in the gullies of the high peaks.
A god-forsaken hole you'd think.
Yet something in its emptiness,
The very aridity of the place,
Called to the Desert Fathers,
Determined to rid themselves
Of both pomp and prelate,
And discover the solace
To be found in time's
Twin antagonists:
Solitude and
Silence.

SAM DAVIDSON

Möbius

Is mind alone the source of its perception?
What then does it perceive? By what conception
Was something made? Was it born of nothing?
If air were empty, what would I be breathing?

Of zero there is nothing, physics proves
And nothing can be said, until it moves
(After eternity that has no span)
Impossibly to one, so time began

With a miracle, from which all flow
Proceeds, its forms declining as they go:
The möbius, symmetrical, complete
Unites the finite with the infinite

With indiscreet discretion, making all
Immaculate, ascending through its fall

HOLLY DAY

Escalation

if I lay still enough
long enough
on the hard-packed snow, on the frozen mud and ice
will my body warm up the ground enough
to trick the tiny seeds
into thinking that it's spring?

If we lie here together
on the same patch of earth
will our combined heat
wake crocuses, make snowdrops unfurl
shake Christmas roses awake
convinced that it's spring?

If you make love to me, here, in the snow
will our bodies melt
enough of this tundra
that tulips and daffodils will race up
through the mud
open bright crowns to herald
an early arrival of spring?

MAREK URBANOWICZ

Lake Semerwater

The sheep are still here
though not the same ones
as when last I came
– relatives perhaps.

It's all relative,
held in a bauble
of time lapsing slow
as the seasons shift,

for what's shifted here
is my eye, blurred now
though the mind behind
the shutter's sharper.

Wind sharpens the blades
of thistles brambling
the decayed church, roof
opened to heaven.

Still a wild haven
for the gloved fox, days
dogged by its living
amidst the grave dead.

The deadly hunt's banned
but still the farmer
sights his rifling eye
on your quarried bones.

I square my boned self
to breathe in the round:
church, sheep, grass, dale, sky,
the purled gold below.

The lake's pearl shimmers,
caught by my lensed eye,
a flung jewel strung
between beaded becks

beckoning the light
of moon, star or ghost
to sheen the water,
stall the steep season.

ANNA FLEMMING

Not a mountain

I am not a mountain

I am lichen and stone,
water and ice, eagles and
sphagnum; hares, birch,
ptarmigan, lynx.

Without salmon
and deer, rowan and heather;
plover, wolf, wind,
pine

I am not a mountain.

Tall and jagged, vast and wild,
I may look like a mountain –

but my skin is stretched thin

flanks turn
deathly green.

You who feast on simplicity
worship a shadow

I am not a mountain

Come gorge on our loss.

ROBIN FORD

What You Don't See When You Look At Me

in a wild wood   once mined
for lead and coal I stumble on an entrance into earth
pick my way along rust rails
past spoil heaps   smoothed
by rain-seep   dark moss   edge
of a cold white stream   where
jaws of rock might crush me

I taste earth-deep   wonder like
a fool if   further in   I might find
arteries of gold   my blood slows
to the deepest pulse

I have also seen stone circles   tombs
on northern islands   wind whine
sea fowl at requiem

               flip the coin

sun-scathed hillside   old city wounded
earthquake-wrecked   fallen courts and temples
tourists   including me   attend
the afterlives of civilisations
stone strewn   silent   hawk-haunted

I walk a broad highway along a ridge
above the modern scrabbled town
past groves of holm oak too dense
for any plant to thrive beneath

we the living pass graves and monuments

    quietly   with purpose   absorbed
        soft spoken
careful not stir the dead

breezes rise   shake oaks softly

        yes
and sometimes I walk in a forest
hear different trees at whisper
feel my feet take root
the sacred earth holding me

BRIGID SIVILL

Rishi Valley

where neem trees filter air
and scorpions scuttle at their roots
I walk with a white umbrella
through the sweltering heat.

Krishnamurti's library, white windows,
stone wall, is a pool of silence.
A photo shows him walking
with a white umbrella
under smaller neem trees than today.

The great banyan tree where he renounced
his destiny as son of God, still hangs its roots
from branches far above the ground. I sit where he sat,
waiting for my shell to crack, smelling the mangoes,
hearing cows shuffling in their shady stalls.

I imagine the white umbrella
dropping slow puffs of air,
sense his breath cleaning my head.
I am open to heat, silence,
the parrot's squawk turning me inside out.

Shanta tells me they sat at his feet
in the hall. 'His words pinned us to the ground.
Like opening a box of rose petals
his drift unfolded us.'

CHRISTOPHER MEREDITH

Sound of leaves not falling

    Out of unmoving air
a handful of the millions
       fell.

      You held your breath
           and tried to hear
                what stirred them.

      Nothing.

Then the bloodlit panes
     not falling
         tinked and clicked in
    choral
      sighing
and became the cipher of the unheard
                   world

       holding
       still
         the tune
of the about-to-be

      like rain
     beginning.

Upstairs

Several lives later
before the last was cleared
I climbed the narrow stairs again.

And there were just the two rooms after all.
Long years I'd dreamed or half-remembered three –
You'd think them needful for so many dead,
crowded, in the skull,
with solving treasure packed in trunks,
on smokebloomed shelves.

In the first, mean room
just long enough for lying down –
a standing crowd of zimmer frames,
her incontinence pads all packeted and stacked.
In the other, more of the same,
and a plain bed unslept in these ten years
still turned down,
two frail wardrobes, bare.

Something in us builds imaginary rooms
the walls somehow exhaling truth
a rippled glass reflecting
a familial face.
And on the battlements must be a ghost,
mustn't there, with a remembered voice
articulating things unsaid
in life,
stilled deepnesses made quick and new?

Onto the dust still landing I dragged a chair
and climbed

and prised up the flimsy attic trap
and peered in
looking for stored elucidations.

But there were mantled joists.
A cranium scraped clear.

She had known a time had come
to tidy up as best you can
and turn and leave.

A chairleg creaked. Dirt furred my hand.

And I could think of nothing
but a steep path down a cliff
all rock and light and moving air
and at its end
the sea.

ROGER GARFITT

The Assyrian Moth

He might be guarding a temple
in Persepolis, this half-inch of husk
on the window sill, such is the stance,

the shoulders rising into spread wings
and the front leg poised, as if to say,
Beware! I'm about to land in all

my majesty! It's like a nod across
the species to see that drive,
the hunger that had brought him

from a nub in the Triassic, from
millennia as jaws in the soil
to the tunnelling through leaves

and the flyting of man and moth,
co-corruptor with rust, *not a whit wiser
for the words he had swallowed.*

He has a nerve! Spread wings
I would resist on a banner, even
on a cap badge, snatch me back

into the centuries of wool and
parchment where I see my own strut
and drudge, from handprints in red ochre

to the hauling of sarsen stones. Plucky
little beggars, weren't we? Who have
to take our teeth out of the tapestry

if there's to be a tapestry at all.

SAM GARVAN

Tumulus

Winter still coursing in the wind
                          and the sky white

Bare thorn hedges

No-one around,
        only a far-off chime of hooves
                somewhere beyond the wood

The field empty,
                thistle and clumped grass

Then on a rise five trees half-made a ring
whitebeam, soft with leaf,
       marking their own season,
vast slabs tilting in the grass
        studded with moss
                inscribed with lichen's ancient lettering.

And when we left, climbing the gate again,
         there was the horse going past
              the colour of weather

A woman riding
         stretching her hand towards the hedge

Riding this way perhaps through all the lanes
        stretching her hand
                summoning

DAVIDE TRAME

What the Thunders Say

Theirs is an ancient solemnity and Tiresias'
memory, weaving our own confession,
and for me an awe that has always come
from up there, from the cluster like grapes
of dark, pregnant clouds.
But after the transfixing lightning bolts
and the pelting rain, the rumbles
just spread as if drawing a necklace,
then their belt of airy, stony roaring
settles in the late afternoon
and lies down in the violet twilight
in the evening, soon.
We are here, all over, they say,
meditating our veins and I sense
assistance in a way, on the swarming
solitude of the land, and a nursing from the
sky
that has grown within me since a child.
Now I dare feel I can come to terms
with their dragon, the blues of their tail-
dragger,
all over the rocks up there, with those vast
fingering flashes swooping here with sky
lashes.
When my time comes I would like my soul
to soar into the trailing roar and find
a berth in one of the nooks and crannies,
the hieroglyphics of their backbone.

The Sacred

Just a thought for me, nothing more,
or the flash of a warm way that anyway
doesn't last much in the streaming
light of the day.
As when reading by chance a novel
touching the Mystery of the Cross
and feeling how much, since childhood,
we have been imbued with this image,
merging with it, I found myself thinking
of crosses ineluctably crossing seas and ages.
But I have always hardly believed in the Resurrection
although I willingly touch the wood of a cross
and the sign of the cross comes to me,
while my feet crunch the gravel of the graveyard,
as if a butterfly were alighting and fluttering
from my brow to my breast in a slight breath.
Well, I am feeling that the sacred is not a thought
after all, but only a flicker with a swarming lightness
and a shiver in which for an instant everything makes
sense.

TOM GOUTHWAITE

A Wish Unmeasured

    Each breath for him,
    each morsel for
    his floating bones,

    each fresh recall
    a relish of
    your care,

    a wish unmeasured
    for his skin, the scent
    and sound of him,

    his first affirming
    moist demand
    for milk.

    Time left your
    breath alone
    beyond the waters,

    no hand
    to touch or hold
    his afterlight

    yet, in your
    bladed clarity
    of open heart,

a fusion deeper,
closer still,
than presence.

Zac's Oak

For Mary

Young stars could see you planting it
inside the wood, their light as rain
for all the years he might have known.

One sapling in a chosen glade
will stand brave emblem for the boy
whose life, by your devotion here,

still grows a grace of stronger boughs
and shadowed summer light, still breathes
a breath of stomata and stars.

Transatlantic Vaughan: The Afterlife of the Silurist in Early American Periodicals[1]

HOLLY FAITH NELSON

'It is but an imperfect bible for Christendom in which the best words of John Bunyan and John Milton, of Henry More and Henry Vaughan... have no place.'[2]

With new humanities databases appearing at a remarkable rate and the rapid growth of the field of digital humanities, reproductions of early modern manuscripts and printed texts have never been more accessible. It is true that these databases cannot reproduce many aspects of the original artefacts given the nature of digitization. We inevitably lose the distinct, multi-sensory experience of interacting with the original material work, engage with the texts in new reading environments, and interpret them differently since new technologies of production and consumption alter how we assign meaning to texts. Nevertheless, humanities databases serve an invaluable supplementary role, inasmuch as they stand alongside and add to our encounters with the original work, and when such encounters are not possible, they grant us access to a version of the otherwise inaccessible original.

---

[1] An earlier version of this article appeared in *Love, Knowledge and the University*, ed. John S. North (Waterloo, ON: North Waterloo Academic Press, 2014), pp. 91-106. The revised version is published with permission.
[2] O.B. Frothingham, 'The Religion of Humanity', *The Radical* 10.6 (April 1872), pp. 256-72 (p. 261), ProQuest –American Periodicals; this database was used to access all of the early American articles cited in this paper.

Transatlantic Vaughan

These databases have played a critical role in my research on the earliest transatlantic crossings of the works and reputation of Henry Vaughan. ProQuest's American Periodicals Series has been of particular use, given its inclusion of more than 1100 periodicals published in America between 1741 and 1940. Since Vaughan, like John Donne, was largely side-lined in the eighteenth century,[3] we must begin with the presence of Vaughan's writings, as well as writings on Vaughan, in the nineteenth-century, 'the first sixty years' of which has been called 'the golden age of American periodicals'.[4] The nineteenth century is of particular importance to Vaughan studies, since it was during this period that Vaughan's reputation as a significant early modern religious poet first took shape, leading to his inclusion in the Anglo-American literary canon, albeit as a minor poet, in the twentieth- and twenty-first centuries.

The afterlife of Vaughan in nineteenth-century America came about in a number of ways, including: the export of three major editions of his works to America and the reprinting of one of these editions three times in Boston; the advertising of editions of his work in American periodicals; the review of

---

[3] No references to Henry Vaughan (the Welsh poet) appear, for example, in Gale's digital collection Eighteenth Century Collections Online.

[4] Introduction to ProQuest's American Periodicals Series, https://proquest.libguides.com/americanperiodicals/apsconstruction.
The phrase 'the golden age of periodicals' appears to date from the April 1831 number of the *Illinois Monthly Magazine* ('From the Periodical Archives', *American Periodicals: A Journal of History, Criticism, and Bibliography* 14.1 [2004], pp. 113–42 [p. 113]). It reappears in 1840 in *The New-York Mirror*, according to Susan Belasco Smith and Kenneth M. Price, 'Introduction: Periodical Literature in Social and Historical Context', *Periodical Literature in Nineteenth-Century America*, ed. by Price and Smith (Charlottesville: University of Virginia Press, 1995), pp. 3–16 (p. 5).

books that include sections on Vaughan in American periodicals; the printing of selected Vaughan poems in American periodicals and books; and the publication of literary criticism on his life and works in the same American media. Vaughan's place in nineteenth-century periodical culture rather than the printed book will be the subject of this first study of 'transatlantic Vaughan' because, as is often noted, 'the periodical' 'shaped the tastes and reading-habits of an emerging mass audience' in Victorian America.[5] In describing the transatlantic journey of cultural objects more generally, the editors of *Robert Burns and Transatlantic Culture* explain that 'cultural objects traverse the Atlantic and map onto North American culture through multiple points of entry', and in the case of Vaughan, the periodical is the dominant point of entry given its wide circulation and affordability.[6]

Susan Belasco Smith and Kenneth M. Price explain that the 'decades between the 1830s and the 1890s transformed the American literary marketplace' due to 'technological developments in papermaking, the widespread use of the cylinder press, cheaper postal routes, rising literacy rates, and wide distribution by railroad'.[7] 'By the 1870s', they continue, 'the inexpensive weekly magazines, an estimated 4,295 of them, had a combined circulation of 10.5 million, a staggering figure given the fact that the population of the United States was only

---

[5] Knowledge Networks: Nineteenth Century American Periodicals, Print Cultures and Communities, Department of American and Canadian Studies, University of Nottingham, https://knowledgenetworks.wordpress.com/.
[6] Sharon Alker, Leith Davis and Holly Faith Nelson, introduction to *Robert Burns and Transatlantic Culture*, ed. by Alker, Davis, and Nelson (Aldershot: Ashgate, 2012), pp. 1–15 (p. 7).
[7] Smith and Price, 'Introduction', p. 3.

30 million in 1870'.[8] Candy Gunther Brown provides more detail about American periodical production and consumption during this century:

> [T]here were perhaps 5000–6000 periodicals founded during the first quarter of the nineteenth century, 2,500 from 1850 to 1865, and 4,300 in the 1870s [...]. The average life expectancy for any paper ranged somewhere from two to four years, with the longevity of papers increasing slightly as the century progressed. As of 1850, there were roughly 600 periodicals in print, nearly one-third of which claimed a religious affiliation.[9]

When we examine the poems of, and literary criticism on, Vaughan in the nineteenth-century periodicals included in ProQuest's American Periodicals Series, a very clear picture emerges of the Vaughan that the typical American reader of religious, literary, political, and socio-economic periodicals would come to know. It should be kept in mind that a significant number of the poems, notes, reviews, articles and the like published in American periodicals first appeared in their British counterparts, and American periodicals sometimes reprinted the content of other American periodicals, hence the tendency to generate a more homogeneous treatment of a given

---

[8] Smith and Price, 'Introduction', p. 5; Smith and Price rely on statistics from Robert E. Spiller et al, *Literary History of the United States*, 3rd ed. (New York: Macmillan, 1963), pp. 805–06.
[9] Candy Gunther Brown, *The Word in the World: Evangelical Writing, Publishing, and Reading in America, 1789–1880* (Chapel Hill: University of North Carolina Press, 2004), p. 154.

subject.[10] In ProQuest's American Periodicals Series, all or part of Vaughan's poems appear as stand-alone pieces 51 times in 32 different periodicals. The same poems appear multiple times, with only 18 different poems appearing in whole or in part between the years 1823 and 1899. All but one of these 18 poems are taken from *Silex Scintillans* (1655); the other one ('To the best, and most accomplish'd Couple'), an epithalamium, appears in the first volume of Vaughan's secular verse: *Poems, with the Tenth Satire of Juvenal Englished* (1646). Of the 18 poems reproduced, seven appear more than once: 'Rules and Lessons'; 'They are all gone into the world of light…'; 'Peace', 'The Rain-bow'; 'Son-Dayes'; Joy of my life! While left me here' and 'As time one day by me did pass'.[11] 'Rules and Lessons' is by far the most reproduced, appearing 22 times. 'They are all gone into the world of light', is reproduced five times, 'Peace' four times, 'Son-Dayes' and 'Joy of my life!' three times each, and 'The Rainbow' and 'As time one day by me did pass' twice each.

That 'Rules and Lessons' in any form would be the most popular Vaughan poem at any time in history may surprise modern readers. In our times, this poem is rarely, if ever, read or anthologized. It is the longest poem in *Silex Scintillans*, reaching 144-lines, and is temporally structured from morning to night. The moral and spiritual behaviour that should be exhibited each day is the focus of the poem, which culminates in the warning that if we fail to '*Love God*' and our '*neighbour*' and to '*watch, and pray*', we will lose '*Heaven's* way' and

---

[10] When editors of American periodicals indicate that they reproduced an article from another magazine, newspaper, etc., that information will be included in the footnotes below.

[11] The other 11 poems are 'The Retreat'; 'The Night'; 'The Pursuit'; 'Cheerfulness'; 'Easter Day'; 'Christ's Nativity'; 'H. Scriptures'; 'The Agreement'; 'To the best, and most accomplish'd Couple'; 'The Seed Growing Secretly'; and 'The Incarnation, and Passion'.

Transatlantic Vaughan

'change' the light of God '[f]or *chains* of *darkness*, and *eternal nights'*.[12] The poem is, to cite Stevie Davies, a 'versified compendium of pious advice'.[13] The politics of civil war and its aftermath are also obliquely embedded in the poem here and there, when Vaughan writes, for example,

> To God, thy country, and thy friend be true,
> If *priest*, and *people* change, keep thou thy ground.
> Who sells Religion, is a *Judas Jew*,
> And, oaths once broke, the soul cannot be sound.[14]

The royalist Vaughan reminds us on more than one occasion that he will not be a sell-out to the Cromwellian regime.

However, the whole poem is only once reproduced in its entirety and with its actual title in nineteenth-century American periodicals included in the database. The other 21 times (the first in 1823 and the last in 1897) it appears, it is untitled or given a different title. The favourite reworked title is 'Early Rising and Prayer.' In these 21 cases, all or some of only the first 36 lines are reproduced, but they are presented as the whole poem. In three cases, instead of part of the original poem, a version 'modernized' by the English Quaker poet and hymn writer Bernard Banton (1784-1849) is offered up. All of the abridged versions of 'Rules and Lessons' focus on spiritual life in the mornings when we should walk with our 'fellow-creatures' and keep our eyes firmly focused on God; the political content is removed.[15]

---

[12] *Henry Vaughan: The Complete Poems*, ed. by Alan Rudrum (Harmondsworth: Penguin Books, 1976; rev. 1983), p. 196. Hereafter cited as *R*.
[13] Stevie Davies, *Henry Vaughan* (Bridgend: Seren, 1995), p. 106.
[14] *R*, p. 193.
[15] *R*, p. 193.

This version of 'Rules and Lessons' was probably appealing from the 1820s onward for three reasons. First and most banal, it initially appeared in the British periodical the *Christian Remembrancer* and was simply reproduced in the *Philadelphia Recorder* on 18 October 1823 and caught on with the public.[16] Second, early nineteenth-century Americans retained a strong sense of personal piety and moral duty associated with their early modern Puritan ancestors and the poem offers up advice on 'holy living' and the 'day's duties.'[17] Praise of the poem in *Russell's Magazine* in May 1857 stresses Vaughan's ability to make this aspect of the poem imaginatively vibrant:

> 'Rules and Lessons' – notwithstanding its prosaic title – is a singularly striking production. While containing an epitome of the 'whole duty of man', it is not coldly philosophic like Pope's 'Essay', but burns with imaginative vitality. Only a true Poet and philosophic thinker could have written it.[18]

Third, the association of spiritual observance and the natural world in the early lines of the poem – including advice to listen to 'the *hush* / And *whispers*' of non-human creation, which prove 'each *bush* / And *oak* does know *I AM*' – resonates with the Romantic and Transcendentalist association of spirit and nature.[19] The spirit, for the Romantics, was revealed through nature, as it is in 'Rules and Lessons', just as, for American

---

[16] 'Early Rising and Prayer', *Philadelphia Recorder* 1.29 (18 October 1823), p. 120.
[17] The poem, called 'Day's Duties', was published in the *Christian Register and Boston Observer* 22.31 (5 August 1843), p. 1.
[18] 'The Sacred Poems, and Private Ejaculations of Henry Vaughan', *Russell's Magazine* 1.2 (May 1857), pp. 191-92 (p. 192).
[19] R, p. 193.

Transatlantic Vaughan

transcendentalist poets, 'natural phenomena' were read 'as symbols of higher spiritual truths'.[20]

The path taken by Vaughan's poem 'The Rain-bow' in nineteenth-century American periodicals – the first 18 lines of which are twice presented as if they were the whole lyric – is similar to that of 'Rules and Lessons.' It is abbreviated in such a way as to stress the role of natural elements, such as a rainbow, in spiritual experience: it reminds us of 'the Covenant 'twixt *All* and *One*'.[21] This version of the 'Rain-bow' excises the original's dark, apocalyptic, and political elements to render it a more Romantic or Transcendentalist piece, one that articulates a kind of spiritual naturalism. Nonetheless, the appearance of poems such as 'Son-dayes' in these periodicals highlights that early American readers recognized that Vaughan's spirituality was of a decidedly Christian character.

Vaughan's spelling of 'Son-dayes' not only reminds us of his Christ-centred faith but also of the fact that he could not attend church (on Sundays) during the Interregnum, hence his focus on encounters with the Son of God in nature. Vaughan's punning title, however, is almost always replaced in nineteenth-century American periodicals with the more ecclesiastical day-of-the-week 'Sunday' or with the more biblical 'Sabbath Days', and the content of the poem is significantly altered to render it less metaphysical, unsurprising in an age that viewed metaphysical elements in early modern poetry as disfiguring.[22]

---

[20] Chris Baldick, 'Transcendentalism', *The Oxford Dictionary of Literary Terms*, 3rd ed. (Oxford: Oxford University Press, 2008), pp. 339–40 (p. 339).
[21] *R*, p. 275.
[22] When Vaughan's poetry is criticized in nineteenth-century American periodicals, a rare occurrence, it is when it is viewed as 'occasionally deformed with the conceit of his time' ([John Brown], 'Henry Vaughan – and Some Later Poets', *The Eclectic Magazine of Foreign Literature*

In the *Christian Secretary*, a version of 'Son-dayes' (under the name 'Sabbath Days') is briefly introduced as 'good poetry' because of its scriptural sentiment and the beauty of its 'diction', though much of the diction is not, in fact, Vaughan's.[23] Fortunately, when the poem was reprinted in *Home Magazine* in 1854, the original text was reproduced in full, alerting American readers to its spiritual and poetic sophistication, and its comfortable synthesis of natural and spiritual experience. 'Son-days' are often figured in 'green' terms in this definition poem, as a 'Transplanted Paradise', '[t]he cool o' the day', '[t]he creatures' *Jubilee*', 'man on those hills of myrrh, and flowers', '[a] gleam of glory, after six-days-showers', 'the combs, and hive, / And home of rest', and '[t]he milky way chalked out with suns'.[24]

The popularity of Vaughan's ecologically-inflected pious poems suggests that editors of American periodicals in this period were drawn to lyrics by Vaughan that would facilitate holy living, encouraging readers to follow their Christian duty throughout the day, to seek God in nature, and to enjoy 'Heaven once a week' at church. But the poems reproduced in these periodicals also suggest that Vaughan was sometimes read in more emotive, even sentimental, terms, particularly with respect to his deeply personal poems on confronting and coping with the pain of a loved one's death. The second most-popular poem by Vaughan published in ProQuest's nineteenth-century American periodicals is an untitled one with a pilcrow or paragraph mark over it. Its first line reads: 'They are all gone into the world of light.' It is variously called, in the periodicals, 'The World of Light', 'They Are All Gone', 'Heaven in

---

17.4 [August 1849], pp. 468-81 [p. 472]); previously published in *The North British Review*.
[23] 'Sabbath Days', *Christian Secretary* 2.10 (24 May 1839), p. 4.
[24] R, p. 205.

Transatlantic Vaughan

Prospect', 'The Glorified', and 'Gone Before.' Only seven of the 10 stanzas are generally presented as the whole poem, though in 1850 the full poem was published in its entirety in the *Christian Register*. To exclude the last three stanzas is to avoid one dense metaphysical section and Vaughan's desperate call for death if God does not 'disperse' the 'mists, which blot and fill' his 'perspective', a sentiment that might have disrupted the common view of Vaughan as a generally hopeful man and writer.[25]

'They are all gone into the world of light' is described by periodical critics as 'one of the sweetest and divinest songs of immortality that have ever been written to comfort and uplift the mourner's heart' and an account of 'an hour of blessed communion with the souls of the departed' by which 'the sweet poet Henry Vaughan [...] made death lovely'.[26] As with Vaughan's other pilcrowed poems, it contains heart-rending reflections on his grief at the death of his brother and wife, among others. And yet it is this painfully personal dimension that renders it significant to the American periodical reader as both the suffering he associates with the death of loved ones and the joy that comes with remembering their presence and looking forward to joining them are universal experiences. The poem was seen both to comfort and instruct. Even two stanzas from it were viewed as sufficient to convey to fretful children the beauty of death, the hope of the resurrection, and the mystery of eternal life, revealed in the aphoristic version of the poem published in 1890 in *The Youth's Companion*:

---

[25] *R*, p. 247.
[26] 'The Literature of Youth, Art. XI: *Memoir of Robert Wheaten*', *The North American Review* 79.164 (July 1854), pp. 239-50 (p. 248); 'The Souls Departed', *The National Magazine* 5 (July 1854), pp. 73-74 (p. 73).

GONE BEFORE.

Dear, beauteous Death! The Jewel of the Just,
  Shining nowhere, but in the dark;
What mysteries do lie beyond thy dust,
  Could man outlook that mark!

He that hath found some fledged bird's nest may know,
  At first sight, if the bird be flown;
But what fair dell or grove he sings in now,
  That is to him unknown.
                           – Henry Vaughan[27]

That Vaughan's more personal elegiac poems resonated so deeply with American readers is evidenced by the fact that three of his most popular lyrics in nineteenth-century American periodicals are pilcrowed poems. 'Joy of my life, while left me here!' and 'As time one day by me did pass' thematically complement 'They are all gone into the world of light' by meditating on death and the feeling that one has outlived one's own life but must still exist, anticipating the life that is to come. At the end of 'As time one day by me did pass', commonly named 'Time's Book' in the periodicals, Vaughan writes,

> Sleep happy ashes! (blessed sleep!)
>   While hapless I still weep;
>   Weep that I have out-lived
>   My life, and unrelieved
> Must (soul-less shadow!) so live on,
> Though life be dead, and my joys gone.[28]

---

[27] 'Gone Before', *The Youth's Companion* 63.18 (1 May 1890), p. 240.
[28] *R*, p. 279.

Transatlantic Vaughan

One can imagine voracious consumers of Charles Dickens's novels in Britain and America (devastated by the death of Little Nell in *The Old Curiosity Shop*) sentimentalizing and universalizing the substance of Vaughan's pilcrowed poems, rather than focusing on the historical reality of war and death that contributed to the elegiac idiom of such lines.

However, the interest in Vaughan's poem 'Peace' in the nineteenth-century American periodical returns us to matters of war and history. Written in the aftermath of the British civil wars, 'Peace' focuses on heavenly peace, which exists above the 'noise and danger' of this world.[29] While it once appears as a stand-alone piece in 1852, it takes on greater significance after the conclusion of the American civil war (1861–1865), when it is printed an additional three times, twice in the 1870s. It was published in the *Advocate of Peace* in early 1877 at the end of a letter to the editor. The editor prefaces the letter and poem thus: 'The following letter from a gentleman who served as a captain in the army during our late civil war, and who has witnessed the scenes of battle and hospital, gives valuable testimony concerning the emptiness of the pomp of war'.[30] The author of the letter tells us that he found in his 'scrap-book' Vaughan's 'Peace' and felt he must reproduce it here because now is the time that it 'should go the "grand rounds" again'.[31]

That Vaughan's writings had this kind of relevance and weight is also evidenced by the fact that American creative writers, including Henry Wadsworth Longfellow and Sarah Hammond Palfrey, used lines from Vaughan's poems ('Rules and Lessons', 'Son-Dayes', 'They are all gone into the world of light', and 'To His Books') as epigraphs to their works between

---

[29] *R*, p. 185.
[30] Agitator [Pseud.], 'Pomp of War', *Advocate of Peace* 8.1 (January / February 1877), pp. 6-7 (p. 6).
[31] Agitator, 'Pomp of War', p. 7.

1839 and 1889.[32] For example, in January 1839, Longfellow published two poems in *The Knickerbocker* – 'The Reaper and the Flowers' and 'The Light of Stars' – under the headings 'A Psalm of Death' and 'A Second Psalm of Life' respectively – both prefaced by a stanza from Vaughan's poetic meditation on death, loss, and longing: 'They are all gone into the world of light.'[33] Longfellow's self-styled 'psalms' on the beauty of death and human resilience in the face of suffering are informed by Vaughan's poetic figuration of psychological pain and spiritual possibility, the disquiet of 'dull and hoary' days without those we love, and the mystical beauty of momentary glimpses of the 'world of light' to which the 'Father of eternal life' has taken them.[34] More than three decades later, Palfrey, a poet and novelist who frequently published under the name 'E. Foxton', borrowed lines from 'Rules and Lessons',

> The sun now stoops, and hastes his beams to hide
> Under the dark, and melancholy earth.
>   All but preludes thy end[,][35]

for the epigraph to her Christmas poem 'Paratus et Fidelis' ['Prepared and Faithful'], published in *The Religious Magazine*

---

[32] In a letter dated 14 August 1868 to James Russell Lowell, Longfellow also obliquely quotes a phrase ('air of glory') from 'They are all gone into the world of light'; see *The Letters of Henry Wadsworth Longfellow, 1866–1874*, ed. Andrew Hilen, vol. 5 (1866-1874) (Cambridge: Harvard University Press), p. 256.
[33] Henry Wadsworth Longfellow, 'A Psalm of Death' and 'A Second Psalm of Life', *The Knickerbocker; or New York Monthly Magazine* 13.1 (January 1839), pp. 13, 77.
[34] *R*, p. 246-47.
[35] *R*, p. 195.

Transatlantic Vaughan

and Monthly Review in December 1870, to underpin her call to be ready for the arrival of Christ.[36]

In Gerard Genette's terms, poets like Longfellow and Palfrey seek to grant themselves 'the consecration and unction of a [...] prestigious filiation', allowing Vaughan's words to serve as an interpretive framework for their own.[37] This growing recognition of the value of Vaughan's spiritual poetry may explain why, between the 1870s and 1890s, we see the publication of a greater number of Vaughan's poems in American periodicals. Versions of 'The Night', 'The Retreat', 'To the Holy Bible, 'H. Scriptures', 'The Incarnation, and Passion', 'Cheerfulness', and 'The Seed Growing Secretly' are first published as self-standing texts within this time frame, if only once each.

This growing appreciation of the works of Vaughan in nineteenth-century American periodicals was also due to his presence in the literary histories and criticism published or republished in dailies, weeklies, quarterlies, and monthlies. There are at least 24 different pieces published in about 15 different periodicals on Vaughan. Beginning with only one article in the 1830s and two in the 1840s, by the 1890's seven articles that cover some aspect of Vaughan appear, this interest in Vaughan gaining more ground after the publication of H.F. Lyte's edition of Vaughan's poems in 1847, which was

---

[36] E. Foxton [Sarah Hammond Palfrey], 'Paratus et Fidelis', *The Religious Magazine and Monthly Review* 44.6 (December 1870), p. 548-49 (p. 548). Sarah Hammond Palfrey was the daughter of John Gorhen Palfrey, DD. LLD (1796-1881), 'the historian of New England, eminent as a clergyman, an anti-slavery reformer, and an author' (*The New-England Historical and Genealogical Register*, ed. by John Ward Dean, vol. 35 [Boston: Printed by David Clapp & Son 1881; rpt. Bowie, MD: Heritage Books, 1996], p. 308).
[37] Gerard Genette, *Paratexts: Thresholds of Interpretation*, trans. by Jane E. Lewin. (Cambridge: Cambridge University Press, 1997), p. 160.

republished in Boston in 1856 and 1858. This commentary on Vaughan introduces more of his writings to American periodical readers and conveys to this sizable audience their aesthetic merit, philosophical underpinnings, and spiritual value.

There are a few general trends in the literary criticism on Vaughan that appears in nineteenth-century American periodicals, some of which explain why certain of his poems are the most popular. First, Vaughan is often presented as a Platonic or mystical thinker in descriptions or assessments of his works. In 1895, in *Littell's Living Age*, both Vaughan and Herbert are presented as 'mystic[s]' and 'symbolist[s]', by which 'the outward sign, the ordinance, the ornaments of religion were weak and faint foreshadowings of some distant glory, some vast truth dimly understood'.[38] Four years earlier, Vaughan is described in the same magazine as 'one of the first psychical poets' who 'gives us the life of the soul in a world of dreams – dreams of beauty, dreams of purity, dreams of holiness.' In this respect, his poems are equated with the 'songs of Blake'.[39] At times, this mystical quality of Vaughan's verse is linked to his Christian sensibility and he is identified as a 'poet-theolog[ian]' of sorts whose 'deep religious feeling' and 'serene submissiveness of spirit' is inscribed in his poems.[40] Vaughan is admired for the 'deep godliness' of his 'spiritual Christianity'.[41] His 'religion', it is said, 'grows up, effloresces into the ideas and

---

[38] Arthur Christopher Benson, 'The Poetry of Keble', *Littell's Living Age* 206.2662 (13 July 1895), pp. 97-106 (p. 103); previously published in *The Contemporary Review*.
[39] 'Henry Vaughan', *Littell's Living Age* 188.2430 (24 January 1891), pp. 236-40 (p. 239); previously published in *MacMillan's Magazine*.
[40] 'Poet-Theology', *The Monthly Religious Magazine and Independent Journal* 23.3 (March 1860), pp. 189-90 (p. 189); 'Henry Vaughan', *Christian Register* 29.51 (21 December 1850), p. 202.
[41] [Brown], 'Henry Vaughan – and Some Later Poets', p. 475.

forms of poetry as naturally, as noiselessly, as beautifully as the life of the unseen seed that 'finds its way up into the "bright" consummate flower'.[42] At other times, Vaughan's Platonic or mystical sensibility is figured in more general spiritual terms: as 'lofty visions of the "supreme, Beautiful, and Good"'.[43]

Second, Vaughan repeatedly comes to the fore as a proto-Romantic poet of nature. This view of Vaughan does not always harmonize with the more theologically-inflected criticism of his work, since readings of Vaughan as a nature poet do, at times, diverge from readings of him as a 'symbolic' poet who interprets natural entities as 'signs' of a greater spiritual truth, though these views are not mutually exclusive. In fact, in an article reprinted in *The Eclectic Magazine of Foreign Literature* in August 1849, John Brown, the admirer of Vaughan's 'spiritual Christianity', also describes the poet in Romantic terms:

> He seems to have had in large measure and of finest quality, (to use the words of Lord Jeffrey as applied to Shakespeare [...]) that indestructible love of flowers, and odors, and dews, and clear waters, and soft airs, and sounds, and bright skies, and woodland solitudes, and moonlight, which are the material elements of poetry; and that fine sense of their undefinable relation to

---

[42] [Brown], 'Henry Vaughan – and Some Later Poets', p. 475.

[43] This phrase is from a review of Robert Albert Vaughan's *Hours with the Mystics: A Contribution to the History of Religious Opinion*. It is applied to the 'lofty poetical dreams of More, Cudworth, [and] Henry Vaughan' (who are included in a 'company of Platonic mystics') ('*Hours with the Mystics*', *The Eclectic Magazine of Foreign Literature* 39.1 [September 1856], pp. 36-49 [p. 48]; previously published in *The British Quarterly Review*).

mental emotion which is its essence and its vivifying power.[44]

In February 1884, J.C. Shairp also writes of Vaughan's unusual ability to combine the 'mystic longing to see the spiritual side of things [...] with another power which seems quite opposed to it – a faithful eye to see and seize the exact form and features of natural things'.[45] Vaughan's treatment of nature, as well as childhood, frequently results in comparisons with Wordsworth.[46] In June 1890, John G. Dow tells readers of *The Eclectic Magazine* that Vaughan's poem 'The Retreat' 'preludes that of Wordsworth upon the heaven that lies about us in our infancy'.[47] On 24 January 1891, Vaughan is called 'the child of nature', the 'predecessor of Wordsworth, the great high-priest of nature, in more ways than one'.[48] And on 1 July 1893, in a review of J.R. Tutin's edition of Vaughan's secular poems, we are informed that Tutin went so far as to pronounce Vaughan 'the Wordsworth of the seventeenth century'[49]

Third, many literary critics defend and admire the poetic style of this 'Old English poet', arguing that given his aesthetic gifts, he deserves a far wider readership.[50] In 1840, in *Arcturus*, Vaughan is introduced thus, 'we turn to an author who deserves to be better known than many of his contemporaries whose

---

[44] [Brown], 'Henry Vaughan – and Some Later Poets', p. 472.
[45] J.C. Shairp, 'Henry Vaughan, Silurist', *The North American Review* 138.327 (February 1884), pp. 120-37 (p. 130).
[46] Vaughan's writing is also, less frequently, associated with the works of William Blake and Samuel T. Coleridge in the nineteenth-century American periodical.
[47] John G. Dow, 'Poets and Puritans', *The Eclectic Magazine of Foreign Literature* 51.6 (June 1890), pp. 733-39 (p. 736).
[48] 'Henry Vaughan' *Littell's Living Age*', p. 238.
[49] Quoted in 'Poetry and Verse', *The Critic: A Weekly Review of Literature and the Arts* 20.593 (1 July 1893), pp. 4-5 (p. 4).
[50] 'Poet-Theology', p. 190.

Transatlantic Vaughan

names have been lately revived',[51] a sentiment echoed in *Russell's Magazine* in May 1857, in which we read: 'We do not believe that there is a Poet in the English language of the unquestionable ability of Henry Vaughan, who has been so systematically neglected by critics and literary compilers' who have failed to see that he is, at times, 'more natural' than George Herbert and has a greater 'appreciation of harmony'.[52] It is Vaughan's apparent avoidance of metaphysical conceits in favour of 'a straight-forwardness and sincerity', 'a clear manly voice', that makes his writings superior to those of Herbert in the minds of some.[53] Unlike Herbert's poems, Vaughan's devotional lyrics, we are told, have a 'special directness and effectiveness',[54] and despite some of the 'same extravagance which deforms the poetry of his contemporaries', Vaughan is praised for 'a far larger measure of grace, smoothness of transition, self-repression and continuity of thought'; he exhibits 'signs of a natural vigor and freshness which are strange to the artificiality of his age'.[55] The 'stilted sentiments' of Herbert are no match for the 'fluency and sweetness' of

---

[51] 'Old English Books', *Arcturus: A Journal of Books and Opinions* 1.1 (December 1840), pp. 42-68 (p. 44). In the 'Editor's Table', *The Knickerbocker; Or, New York Monthly Magazine* 17.1 (January 1841), pp. 78-90, it is suggested that Evert A. Duyckink, who, along with Cornelius Mathews, edited *Arcturus*, authored 'Old English Books', as it shows his 'cultivated taste and critical powers, as well as an example of his pleasing style' (p. 85).
[52] '*The Sacred Poems, and Private Ejaculations of Henry Vaughan*', *Russell's Magazine* 1.2 (May 1857), pp. 191-92.
[53] 'Old English Books', *Arcturus*, pp. 46, 48.
[54] 'New Editions', *Outlook* 55.1 (2 January 1897), p. 97.
[55] 'Henry Vaughan', *Littell's Living Age*', p. 237.

'Vaughan at his best'.[56] Some critics disagree, but others do not.[57]

There was no writer and literary critic more vocal in Vaughan's defence in nineteenth-century American periodicals and books than Louise Imogen Guiney (1861–1920), the Irish-American poet, essayist, biographer, and editor. In arguing for Vaughan's importance as a writer, she relies on all three of the dominant critical approaches to his works described above, presenting him as a Christian 'nature-mystic', a proto-Romantic, and an accomplished poet, while also revealing the political character of some of his poems.[58] Jonathan Nauman has discovered the sweeping scope of Guiney's original research on Vaughan, arguing that it was inspired in part by 'her Boston royalist enthusiasms', which led her to admire Vaughan's royalist resolve and poetics during the Interregnum, as well as her Catholic faith, which drew her to his anti-Puritan, mystical spirituality.[59] Between 1885 and 1895, Guiney published at least a letter and article on Vaughan in two American periodicals.[60]

In a letter to the editor of *The Critic* in December 1895, Guiney laments the pitiable state of Vaughan's grave in

---

[56] 'Henry Vaughan', *Littell's Living Age*', pp. 239, 240; F.T. Palgrave, 'A Glance at English Hymns Since the Reformation', *Littell's Living Age* 1299 (24 April 1869), pp. 195-203 (p. 197)' previously published in *Good Words*.
[57] In 'Literature – At Home', *Putnam's Magazine* 5.27 (March 1870), pp. 371-77, for example, Vaughan is described as Herbert's superior as a poet: 'Vaughan, as a sacred poet, leaves Herbert an unmeasurable distance behind him' (p. 376). Other nineteenth-century critics simply consider the relative strengths of each poet.
[58] Davies, *Henry Vaughan*, p. 171.
[59] Jonathan Nauman, 'F.E. Hutchinson, Louise Guiney, and Henry Vaughan', *Scintilla* 6 (2002), pp. 135–147 (p. 136).
[60] Guiney also published material on Vaughan in nineteenth-century books, continuing to advocate for the poet in periodicals and books well into the twentieth century.

Transatlantic Vaughan

Llansantffraed in Breconshire, Wales. In attempting to raise funds to repair his grave, Guiney tells her American readers on 28 December 1895 of a letter she published in the English magazine *The Athenaeum* earlier that year, in which she stressed that Vaughan is or was 'a poet dear to Mr. [James Russell] Lowell, Mr. Matthew Arnold, Prof. [F.T.] Palgrave, Dr. John Brown and some other people who honor genius', including H.F. Lyte and Alexander B. Grosart, thereby consecrating Vaughan through affiliation with the British and American literati.[61] In the original letter, she estimates that there are about 'fifty' 'lovers' of Vaughan on both sides of the Atlantic thanks to the efforts of these literary critics.[62] Having raised only part of the needed funds from English lovers of Vaughan, she now calls for transatlantic cooperation if 'a coal-shed' is to be 'moved from the head of his tomb in the churchyard', appealing to American pride along the way: 'If five or six Americans will now contribute five dollars each, it can be done, to the added everlasting credit of our own country, which has so much more thought and tenderness for old English literature than have the English themselves'.[63] An illustration of Vaughan's grave and the offending coal-shed accompanies the letter, showing the power of both image and word in transatlantic cultural memory-making.

A decade earlier, in *The Independent*, Guiney had addressed the problem of cultural forgetting when discussing Vaughan's presence, but marginalization, in the Anglo-American literary canon, claiming that he was a 'persistently neglected' poet,

---

[61] Louise Imogen Guiney, 'Henry Vaughan's Grave', *The Critic: A Weekly Review of Literature and the Arts* 24.723 (28 December 1895), p. 446.
[62] Louise Imogen Guiney, 'The Grave of Henry Vaughan', *The Athenaeum* 3546 (12 October 1895), pp. 492-93 (p. 492).
[63] Guiney, 'Henry Vaughan's Grave', p. 446.

despite the fact that '[a]nthologies now receive[d] him into their select circles.'[64] Guiney believed that by 1885 Vaughan was only anthologized 'with courtesy, scarce with enthusiasm', and the limited literary criticism on Vaughan's writings at this time appears to bear out her claims.[65] Her reflections on and defence of the poetry of Vaughan in 'A Forgotten Voice' are nothing less than a call to arms, made clear in an excerpt from that manifesto:

> Has no one found out how much he knew of his art, and how reverently he served it? How he came, both by nature and by grace, to some exquisite terseness and surety of expression? Or how he stood, in his equable, sweet, reticent genius, as near to greatness, for instance, as our own Longfellow, who was indubitably like him? His eulogies are all to be sung; and, meantime, we know that depreciation can never approach him again [...]. Let it be written of Henry Vaughan, sometime rhymer in merry England, that men long forgot him in their annals, and they who alone were mindful, undervalued him; that his memory, downtrodden with the sods of his old inland grave, had yet a sweet fragrance after two hundred years; and that then a casual comer, least of his friends, abashed to have known him so tardily and so lightly, made bold to break a

---

[64] Louise Imogen Guiney, A Forgotten Voice', *The Independent [...] Devoted to the Consideration of Politics, Social and Economic Tendencies, History, Literature and the Arts* 37.1908 (25 June 1885), pp. 3-4 (p. 3)
[65] Guiney, 'A Forgotten Voice', p. 3.

Transatlantic Vaughan

lance with those in authority for his sake and for truth's. *Adorum qui feci* [I did the deed].[66]

In her role as Vaughan's defender, Guiney actively circulated his name and sanctioned his writings through periodical culture in the late nineteenth century and beyond. Between 1894 and 1897, her research, work in progress, or publications on Vaughan were remarked upon or reviewed in a range of American periodicals, including *The Literary World, The Book Buyer, The Critic, The Dial,* and *The Bookman*. Without the joint efforts of Guiney and her colleague, the Welsh politician, antiquary, and author Gwenllian E.F. Morgan (1852–1939), there would have been far fewer readers of L.C. Martin's seminal edition of Vaughan's collected works in 1914, far less research material on which F.E. Hutchinson could draw for his influential 1947 biography of Vaughan, and far fewer academic monographs and articles on Vaughan published in the twentieth century.[67]

In the twenty-first century, scholarship on Vaughan has paid particular attention to the political nature of his writings, texts produced in the shadow of a brutal civil war that left Vaughan feeling as if he were a psychological and spiritual exile in this world. In the nineteenth-century American periodical, this aspect of Vaughan is merely touched upon and only after the American civil war. Perhaps it is not surprising in light of the wars across the globe, and the ongoing 'War on Terror', in the twentieth and twenty-first centuries that we look to

---

[66] Guiney, 'A Forgotten Voice', pp. 3-4.
[67] As Nauman succinctly puts it, Guiney and Morgan, 'can fairly be ranked as the most important pioneers in early twentieth-century Vaughan studies' ('F.E. Hutchinson, Louise Guiney, and Henry Vaughan', p. 135). This article has sought to confirm that Guiney's pioneer work began in the previous century.

Vaughan's works to hear the voice of a war-weary poet seeking a different world or alternative home. But in our (post)modern world, Vaughan's hopeful words on a 'world of light' and an everlasting 'glory' often fall on deaf ears.[68] Nevertheless, like the producers and consumers of nineteenth-century American periodicals, we too are part of this story of re-shaping and re-evaluating the works of Vaughan in our own image. And in studying the early years of 'transatlantic Vaughan' through new digital technologies, we have the opportunity to revisit the deeply contextual nature of our own readings of, and responses to, early modern literature.[69]

---

[68] *R*, p. 246.
[69] Thanks are due to my research assistant Natalie Anne Boldt, for her exceptional work on collecting and collating the primary sources for this study.

Twenty-four Swans
by Ann Lewis

MARTIN HAYDEN

A Journey to Make, Sometime

For David, on Iona

Leave the village by the cart track:
it runs along beside the hall (you'll not forget
to shut the gate, for errant sheep and cattle).
Climb the slope below the House of Prayer
(if you go for a sojourn in the chapel
I'll be there with you in the silence).
Bend inland to the farm, not minding the dogs:
you'll see the track goes down and up before you
into the island's hilly south. At the crossroads
no angels, corncrakes fussing out of sight
in the grass, crake-crake, crake-crake:
let them speak a while, it'll do you good.
As the ditches either side grow deeper
don't let first primroses much distract:
be busy with the slope, and through the gate
find solid footholds in the hoof-churned mud.
Ignore straight ahead, walk left, go up
over the brow towards the sky, and watch
for a little-used path half-buried in heather
sinuous and black with its toy cliffs:
it'll pull you steadily up into the wind
smarting your eyes, ruffling your ears.
But no, not this top, nor the next,
don't mind the wind just now,
on you go to the sudden viewpoint
where you two turned your backs on Erraid
and the distant headland of the Carsaig Arches,

brothers at one as the rain came on,
improvising for the hell of it
a brief handheld game of cards
with no time for serious winners or losers:
stop there and feel his warmth there too.

MARTIN BENNETT

Alrewas Return

In 2010 a local man chanced upon the Staffordshire Hoard, 1,500 gold and silver items dating from the 7th and 8th centuries.

Back in Offa's heartland, its marl
stashing cross and sword-hilt inlaid
with garnets, the commonest clays
crusting bended fine-etched gold,
I stroll, a latter-day housecarl –

Bone-bound of old each dread marauder,
rust for riverbed his spear or blade,
waterways wend millennia –
willow, swan, eponymous alder
to enrich the tread, home the gaze.

Trent-Mersey Canal

Re-aligning shadow,
water's lithe pewters –
how, quick-quick slow,
crinkly lock-cranked flow
works up a thirst,

the same glide and glow
whereby Josiah Wedgwood,
this stretch's progenitor,
once avoided potholed roads,
so saving on cracked crockery.

Milepost starboard shows
3 more to go. Tiller's click;
towpath familiars
Of alder, hawthorn, willow
then in weathered brick

there appears
alongside its quay
his erstwhile depot –
Signing memorial cheers,
'The Swan' at Fradley.

MICHAEL HENRY

Pyromania

Mondrian tracks lead to where
designer gorse has been cut down to stubble.
Voilà, two burnt-out Astras. Someone in my atelier
should preserve them in an installation.

Such beautiful exudations on the bonnets:
a crazing like lichen and a scorched-orange reptile,
aboriginal art from another country where
terracotta, not green, is the predominant colour.

Someone should curate the beauty of stone:
pharaoh's profile raging with sunlight,
sphinx's head on ridge-of-grass haunches,
recumbent limestone grouted with moss.

Someone should point to clouds darkening the sun
that shines a long arm down to Winchcombe
and the singular light of the great mist
that stitches with its own petit point.

Someone in my studio should burn old cars
for the sheer diabolical artistry of it.

Sunny Sands Tribute

All over England they have drawn
portraits of soldiers in the damp sand.

Here, where the cliff is sheer against the shore
and where the kind old sun mints water-coins,
Wilfred Owen swam on his last evening in England,
doing the backstroke perhaps, opening
the papal whites of his eyes to unforgiving sky.

Here, where women watched him
march down the Road of Remembrance,
crowds now plough down the slope
like dogs following a blood trail to see
his dear-achieved portrait in the sand.

Here, where his mouth is, he might have placed
his neatly folded battledress,
and where the parting of his hair is
or his proud regimental tie
he might have placed his polished army-boots.

And here the tenacity of the tide
is watering over every detail of his features
like a celebratory beacon being doused
and everyone's walking back up the street
with his poems like the Lord's Prayer on their lips.

RIC HOOL

Enlightenment

That year
        British Summertime began
           late March
                we leapt forward
sparring-mad hares
        kicking sunlight
at shortening darkness
        Beltaine arresting Imbolc's thrust

Then watched tiger moths
                on July evenings
in hushed discovery   captured
            in moments between decay
Outside of *knowing* we entered
              a changed light

Halfway to Everything

    a clouded moon
    a falling seed

    to live in this world
    exploding slowly
        so gorgeously painful

    courageous with pen in a once empty room
    so crowded now   no space
        to wheel locution

    as much as words are brought to things
            things are brought to
    words

    the persistence of thought   the
        resistance of pulled roots

SARAH LINDON

East

A few miles away, cranes plumb
the sky and work their stitches

so glass can climb like sliding doors
facing back at us, unpicking

the horizon, making unground,
then inviting us to observe

the lowering backdrop and extendable
sky. The old places still exist –

the palace on the hill, the clots
of riverboats, the dense cataracts

floating greenly in the canal,
wandering in submerged vision.

Out in the high air all is lighter
as if indifferent to gravity,

a city of prosthetics. It seems to be
how the future arrives, waiting

for in-breath. Strange fantasies
move through screens and walls

and bodies. The city has learnt
to keep us moving. We slip off it.

Here, buildings rise the colour of rust
as if to blear their claims on space.

A viewing tower forms as spun sugar,
lawns as sharp-edged cosmetics.

We make of houses a concept
glimpsed in magazines or far

countries. But still, flaking walls,
dusty books, cobwebbed panes

with dancing leaves beyond,
lime-scaled kettles, collections

of abandoned pens, make time
a substance. Unreal city,

why do you ignore yourself?
Let the river steer you. A plane

reckons its way in, unsteady
but convinced, screaming and staring.

Like Day and Night, Emerge and Hide

In the notches of land
wood turns, shuffling
shade over dust and
duff and damp earth,
holding its air-hoard
away from the scorch,
the bright of a star
holding a hypnotic
raw glare. Land
is gnarled here, a hand
lined and ridged with
holding the sea
and where it curls,
clefts, and where
it opens, the silky
pale paper of sand.
Here the sea has
pulled back again,
discarded weed congeals,
rock kinks and dries,
grazing the sky.
The earth rides up
the horizon, cliffs
develop stature,
grass mixes its heated
scent with dirt.
Until, turning
like a sleeper surfacing,
water bodies up,
flowing into the touch
of every inlet, every
channel. Salt breathes
inland and valleys

bristle in its sighs.
The swell carries
the whole complement
of liquid light,
pushing and
altering horizons.

SEAN H. MCDOWELL

Photogram

My uncle taught me the inverse of light,
The radiance of shadows and inner
Lives of oak leaves, fern fronds and canning jars.

There in that crypt-like cellar, at the base
Of narrow, rounded stairs fit for a keep,
I was surprised one day to find a darkroom,

And my uncle hard at work, two prints pinned
To a clothesline, fixer and developer
Solutions vinegaring the air.

A safe light suspended from a socket;
Opaque bottles, plastic trays, bamboo tongs
All laid out beside the utility sink;

And the enlarger, that impromptu beast,
A plywood platform, a heron's neck of pipe
And a squat head as wide-eyed as an owl's.

What need had we for old film negatives
When a box of photographic paper
Could open into story like canvas?

My uncle taught me you didn't need much,
A handful of leaves, perhaps – oak, maple.
Scatter a few on a sheet, then shine your light,

And what seeps into clarity beneath
Your gently agitating tongs is not
Mere accident or chance but a vision:

The spotlighted ghosts of leaves, not fallen
But falling, floating free perpetually
In the pure black of elemental night.

Or dive into a coffee dark sea
With daisies, mums and marigolds, once
On fire in that garden on Everett Street,

Now a swimming school of luminous
Invertebrates. See them cluster? Watch them
Wavering at the bottom of a tray.

Or take a pair of chive blossoms, purple
Cupola we snip or pinch to foster
New growth. Flash them for thirty seconds,

And they transform into sparklers arrested
The moment before their bonfires of sparks
Burst into showers with a crackling hiss.

So many still lifes dripping on newsprint.
Yet so much left to do in the apricot
Dimness of that darkroom-for-a-day.

We tried landscapes next – all nocturnes, of course,
The moon as perfect a circle as
The canning jar seal we used to make it.

Call this one *Alpine Crossing*: sprigs of pine,
Cedar and juniper are full-grown trees
Staggered on a moonlit slope in summer.

You want to climb those torch-lit crowns
Out of the dark of every hill of worry
And shine as they do, brighter than stars.

Call this one *Go*: a sleek greyhound
As bright as the moon or X-rayed bone runs
Toward the cellophane snow of a mountain.

So what if it once ornamented the hood
Of a 1930s Lincoln? Now it flies
Forever in the joyride of a chase.

Call this one *The Long Road Home*: it might be
A moonscape if it weren't for the lake,
The roadside fence, cut-out hills and paper duck.

See how the stars are as fine as sugar?
The trees have launched like phosphorus missiles.
That curved road carries you straight to the sky.

But my favorite is another still life:
On a table fashioned from brush fringe,
Long-stemmed Silver Dollars spill from a bottle –

Nothing special and yet so much my uncle
He might as well have signed his name.
Beside the bottle, a pair of duck eggs

Where apples or pears might have glistened
In a mood-lit Renaissance painting.
And in the space above, a cigarette

He plucked from behind his ear. He set it
Alongside the petals where its shadow
Glows diagonally like a U. F. O.

Dried thistle and curling fern, strip of lace
And lavender bloom, oregano and maiden
Grass. Cigarette and lighter, clothespin

And rusty nail, coffee mug and empty jar.
Trickle of the stop bath, slick photograph,
Pat-pat-pat of drops draining onto newsprint.

The thing itself and what imagination
Does to it: my uncle taught me the difference,
And sometimes that difference is all you need.

Driftwood

Driftwood log like a tusk upthrust
or a whale's jawbone erected
to catch late afternoon sun,

you cast long shadows.
You are a cat's promontory
bolted to a carpeted round,

an island on our Canadian ash floor,
a lost object found by saw and drill,
ratchet and bolt. When we hauled you

from the seaside boneyard,
the Pacific had bleached you
to a hoary blonde. Now you live

in two: your other half presides downstairs.
Your rounded top slowly darkens
from the passage of many hands.

When a cat rakes his claws against you,
they hiss like droplets in an oiled skillet.
Yet the flakes you shed are as soft as cork.

NICHOLAS MCGAUGHEY

The Ring

The old ring was lost or stolen,
Bought on the never-never
On the eve of our empty chapel.

This new band has been forged
From many declarations, spilling
From a box of old commitments

To be smelted in a crucible of clasp and chain.
One eternity, a keepsake that lost its charm
And the uncoupled links of a gold wristwatch.

Tokens given at font and altar,
That glowed on clutched pillow and sheet,
To be chucked or soaped-off by morticians…

All the muck of life is veined there in the circle
Of surname and children. A century
Of unions, paper, silver, ruby or gold.

I twist its weight from my finger,
Another ring is left: a transparent tattoo,
Which heals, then disappears too.

WILLIAM VIRGIL DAVIS

For Marie Curie on her 150th Birthday

What is not known?

what she wrote and what she
left behind, taken from her
pockets when she died
and deposited in lead-lined boxes.

What she wanted to be known:

that she was Polish.
that she married Pierre Curie.
that she worked in France.

What should we do?

take an x-ray in an ambulance
on the way to the hospital.

Widow

One day he was there, the next
gone. She stands at the door
and watches up and down.

Rain and wind sweep the street
clean. Even the oldest oaks
bend until it looks like they may

break. She asks herself questions,
and tries to answer them.
No one calls and none will come.

She waits, watching the rain rain.

CLAIRE SCOTT

Foundering

Foundering offshore
in the lick of night
little time on my breath
per Dr. Edward Stanton perusing
the MRIs, the blood tests, the X-rays
I toss cargo over the side
my 2015 Honda my two-story house
with its wrangled rose garden
my DVDs my underwear
send money to Doctors Without Borders
Alameda County Food Bank
to lighten the load
to lessen the chance
no star to lean on
in the beating silence
no myth to slip into
to stave off oblivion

watery pall bearers wait
brushing seaweed from their hair

PAUL MATTHEWS

World Rose

Can any rose since Eden
command our trust?
Its first bud has only
to open in the yard
and every evil seems
forgiven suddenly.

No worm tongue
mars this moment.

Our fitful senses
yield to the scent
and a kindness once
our own instils the blood
strong to undo what
deems the rose unworthy.

Winter's Traces

A king's son once rode
through this High Gate,

and as his bridle bells
thrilled to the chase

fallow deer pricked
their ears in the wood,

and though
he is centuries dead,

his rash blood muted,
I wish snow to cover

every scent and trace
that no innocent thing

be troubled in Ashdown
this quiet Christmas Eve.

NICHOLAS MURRAY

Parbold

In a Lancashire church you left your hat,
its abandonment transformed into a legend.

Why did you not go back? Why did it sit
for ever on a polished bench, unclaimed?

What kind of hat was it? One of your pork-pies
of green tweed with that central crease or fissure?

Or a more stylish trilby, a little forties,
a little *noir*, like the titfer of a private dick

walking the night in his long coat (to strident music)
while the villain gave it wellie in a finned car?

We will be like you, leaving behind stories,
half-finished, puzzling, with no point.

Europe

I call you a lake
on which our boat
(red-white-and-blue)
glides under sail.

The island nation
whose anchor rattles
down-down-down
to a bed of sand.

The same wave
slaps our hull;
the same wind
flaps the jib.

The lake has room
for numerous craft.
Windermere-wide,
it feels fathomless.

We have our quirks,
our captain's jokes.
You mend your nets,
squatting like a tailor

in an old print.
From a quayside cafe
there is laughter
and the chink of glasses.

There is room for all
on the lake's surface;
the far hills at sunset
are bathed in light.

Were it not for the flags
we should not know
one from the other
as the boats skip by.

A Short History of Ethics

Much has been written
on the subject of The Good.
It echoes like a gong

calling us from our sins.
It could be painted
as a bright sun between fronds

of the thrashing sycamore,
a dish of brilliance,
a bright target.

A halo circles it
such as saints wore
in the dark churches

frequented in my youth;
made of tin, tarnished,
but operative as an example.

ANDREW NEILSON

The Week's Remains

What shall I say, when plunging into talk
    across the length of the sofa –
being as we are in Friday's domain,
    when others silence the shofar –
where, to the heralding of *wine o'clock*,
we review our week and what might remain?

There is no horn, for sounding or for drink,
    just these two glasses.
The light they reflect is the glistered cost
    of everything that passes:
the week's work won, another at the brink...
but it's clear, what is won is also lost.

Lessons beyond the daily rigmarole,
    beyond the nine-to-five,
beyond even wars and the migrants camped,
    this sadness we derive
from time, mutability, self-as-soul –
notions with which each of us are stamped.

And yet, if we had no shoes on our feet,
    our city was a shelled-out square –
with a few walls standing almost absently,
    as if to show they *care*;
nothing to fight for, gunfire on the street –
why of course, we would feel quite differently,

as an eye applied to a telescope lens
    fixes on what differs
in those multiplied scales of magnitude.

    Yet all life suffers...
or so we assume, both pensive and tense
and human in our own vicissitude.

How long does luck last? That we cannot know.
    As here, when looking at your face,
I pour into each glass, you say my name,
    and even as our words race,
I wonder how to keep this moment's glow
sheltered like a hand around a flame.

SUSAN SKINNER

December Night at the Stable

Moon silence, horse silence:
She limps in pain to reach
her net of hay.
Inside the row of stables others shift,
turn their soulful eyes

to the girl running towards her own horse.
Time passes. Now
through trees with crooked limbs
a round moon cartwheels, sending
a beam of white light onto the roof

of the stable where the girl
whispers into the horse's twitching ear:
'it will soon be better'.
She lifts the damaged hoof,
washes and binds the wound.

Night batters grey-black wings across the moon,
stable lamps go out
but the girl stays and whispers comfort things
to her horse. In the aloof, starless dark
only her love is light.

On a Beach

It's light weather, light on willow leaves
light dipped in streams, light in waves
of whispering grass,
light on bees' wings, fragile butterflies.

I see you waiting, straw hat tilted, grave
yet jocular, sitting on the raised
bench above the grass and I gaze
hoping you will see me. For this day,

this minute is see-through , the light grazes
and reveals at the same time – the way
a mirror reflects your face, my face
the other side of light and loneliness.

Under the Quarry Woods: journal into prose poetry

JEREMY HOOKER

Over the years I have occasionally written a prose poem but, until quite recently, without much conscious thought of what makes it a prose poem. As a contrast to the work that I shall concentrate on here, *Under the Quarry Woods*, published in 2018, I will begin with a poem that I wrote in the 1970s, which represents a different, and perhaps more conventional, form of prose poetry. 'Matrix' places the Cerne Abbas Giant in the context of his Dorset landscape:

> A memorial of its origins, chalk in barns and churches moulders in rain and damp; petrified creatures swim in its depths.
>
> It is domestic, with the homeliness of an ancient hearth exposed to the weather, pale with the ash of countless primeval fires. Here the plough grates on an urnfield, the green plover stands with crest erect on a royal mound.
>
> Chalk is the moon's stone; the skeleton is native to its soil. It looks anaemic, but has submerged the type-sites of successive cultures. Stone, bronze, iron: all are assimilated to its nature, and the hill forts follow its curves.

Under the Quarry Woods: journal into prose poetry

> These, surely, are the work of giants: temples re-dedicated to the sky god, spires fashioned for the lords of bowmen:
>
> Spoils of the worn idol, squat Venus of the mines.
>
> Druids leave their shops at the midsummer solstice; neophytes tread an antic measure to the antlered god. Men who trespass are soon absorbed; horns laid beside them in the ground. The burnt out tank waits beside the barrow.
>
> The god is a graffito carved on the belly of the chalk, his savage gesture subdued by the stuff of his creation. He is taken up like a gaunt white doll by the round hills, wrapped around by the long pale hair of the fields.[1]

This piece may be seen to correspond to a definition of prose poem given in *The New Princeton Encyclopedia of Poetry and Poetics*: 'high patterning, rhythmic and figural repetition, sustained intensity, and compactness'.[2] I wasn't thinking in these terms at the time of writing, but only concentrating on my subject, and finding words to fit it. 'Matrix' could be realigned to make a more conventional sort of poem, so why this shape on the page?

---

[1] Jeremy Hooker, *Soliloquies of a Chalk Giant* (London: Enitharmon Press, 1974), p. 11.
[2] Alex Preminger and T. V. F. Brogan, *The New Princeton Encyclopedia of Poetry and Poetics* (Princeton: Princeton University Press, 1993), p. 977.

The opening words, 'A memorial of its origins', help to determine its form as a poem that represents the geology and history of its chalk-land site. As 'a shape in words',[3] 'Matrix' unfolds to embody the Giant's landscape, his geological and historical matrix. The shape is formed by images, phrases, sentences, and paragraphs, as if carved out of words by analogy with an earth-work. As a poem resembling a landscape, it doesn't differ essentially from a poem shaped like an altar or an hourglass. Form matches content, and it embodies its theme by bringing together male and female elements to reveal the Giant in his matrix, 'his savage gesture subdued by the stuff of his creation'.

The writing process was largely instinctual. I felt the result was the right shape for the material: a poem set out like a chalk landscape, in which layers of its geological and historical making are embedded. It is a made thing, embodying the Giant's landscape on the page.

'Matrix' is one sort of prose poem, an extremely various form established in France in the nineteenth century, and widely practised since then in Europe, Britain, America and other countries, as the recent *Penguin Book of the Prose Poem* demonstrates. But prose poetry, I would argue, is by no means confined to the prose poem, as a moment's thought about the King James Bible will prove, without reference to modern novelists such as Joyce, Woolf, and Beckett. Prose poetry can be found almost anywhere in the realm of written words.

---

[3] Making 'a shape in words' is an expression I owe to David Jones's Preface to *In Parenthesis* (London: Faber & Faber, 1937), p. x. It seems to me especially appropriate for the prose poem. *In Parenthesis* is the greatest twentieth century work in English to make extensive use of prose poetry. Other notable examples, in English. of sequential prose poems are Roy Fisher's *City*, 1961, and Geoffrey Hill's *Mercian Hymns* (1971).

Under the Quarry Woods: journal into prose poetry

There is, however, a specific kind of writing to which the prose poetry of *Under the Quarry Woods* [4] belongs, and that is the literary journal, diary, or daybook. This is a form that I love, and have called, borrowing from D. H. Lawrence on the novel, 'bright book of life'. I kept a diary when I was a boy, and occasionally as a student, but started what I called a journal in 1969. I have kept this ever since, every few days, if not every day.

Diary-keeping is a habit widely practised. Why? One function is the Pepysian pleasure of talking about oneself. But the literary journal is not so narrowly confined, as we see in, for example, Dorothy Wordsworth, and Coleridge, as well as writers such as Richard Jefferies, Gerard Manley Hopkins and Virginia Woolf, and Thoreau and Emerson in America. I'm aware that, of these, Jefferies has been the principal influence on my writing: on the journal that I've kept for some 50 years, and on the poetry that, to a significant degree, derives from it.

Before returning to closer questioning of reasons for journal or diary keeping, it is necessary to give an idea of what *Under the Quarry Woods* is like, with an extract:

> Goldfinches on a May morning, feeding on dandelion seeds. Climbing the stems, which occasionally give under them, they settle further down, with a flutter of wings, snatching beakfuls of seed, while other seeds, shaken out, float away on the air. Behind them, at the edge of the woods, new leaves seethe in a breeze, surfaces speckled with light. Strands of spider silk shine. Illuminated seeds float across the garden. (*UQW*, p. 6)

---

[4] Jeremy Hooker, *Under the Quarry Woods* (London: Pottery Press Pamphlet number 3, 2018). Where necessary, page references, designated *UQW*, will follow quotations in the text.

SCINTILLA 23

This is the first of three sections on this page; on other pages there are more, or fewer. Each section, or passage, is as long as it needs to be: the length of an observation, or perception, or process of thought. Each is an extract, a piece 'quarried' from the journal, and given its specific shape by editing. This section is an immediate observation of goldfinches feeding on dandelion seeds. What is seen is an active process. It could be described as a visionary moment, with words such as 'shine' and 'illuminated' denoting a sense of the numinous. But this is natural vision, not something worked up. I am wary of contemporary writing that claims to be visionary.

The following section homes in on the historical landscape:

> Fact beggars imagination when I think of Cunarders, *Mauritania & Lusitania*, powered by steam coal from the Deep Navigation, vying for the Blue Riband.
>
> Coal from here lies in *RMS Titanic* on the Atlantic bed.
>
> Here the unseen presses upon the seen, and the ripped land wears a face of unbelievable peace.

'Homes in' is a loose metaphor which suggests the action of a camera. My concern, however, is with the unseen, at least as much with the seen. The writing is about process, not just visual experience, which isolates detail: 'Here the unseen presses upon the seen'. The face of the land intimates what lies under it and has contributed to its making, and to the shaping of an imperial

Under the Quarry Woods: journal into prose poetry

history. A theme of the sequence as a whole emerges here: power, contrasting and interacting natural and human power. As in conventional forms of verse, the prose poetry of *Under the Quarry Woods* works partly by suggestion, and with images.

The third section on this page switches back to a natural scene:

> On the path a peacock suns its open wings. Brimstone on a dandelion, yellow bringing out the gold on the whole flower face. A peacock chases off a bee, as a crow would harry a buzzard.
>
> A faint pulse on a small pond. A moth, almost the same colour as mud on the bottom, drowning. Saved with the tip of my stick. But everywhere among the teeming lives are lonely deaths.
>
> Poets make such a fuss of their self-drama, myself not least; but I find that consciousness at its purest and deepest issues in prayer.

Death as a natural and human fact is common in this former industrial landscape. It enters observation and provokes thought, stimulating some of the more personal reflections. Inevitably, the writing is a form of self-expression. But it presses against limits, transcending the merely personal to seek common ground in fellow feeling and an enlarged sense of Self. As in all my poetry, *Under the Quarry Woods* explores material ground, and seeks a deeper 'grounding', beyond 'self-drama', and in prayer.

Why keep a diary? There are probably as many reasons as there are diarists. I recognise the following in my own writing:

to observe, to record, to remember; to catch something of the quick of life as it passes; to learn to see, and to think. Coleridge spoke of writing as an aid to living an examined life. His grandson, editor of his unpublished notebooks, said that 'from youth to age note-books and pocket-books were [Coleridge's] silent confidants, his 'never-failing friends' by night and day'.[5] A journal can be a conversation with oneself and an aid to self-knowledge. In my case, in teaching me how to see, it has taught me how to write.

If this seems over-solemn, we should remember Anaïs Nin's words: 'We write to taste life twice, in the moment, and in retrospection'.[6] How sharp the taste of life is; how delicious; how bitter; how elusive. As Edward Thomas wrote in 'The Glory': 'I cannot bite the day to the core'. In my *Welsh Journal* I exclaimed: 'Life is now, it is here'.[7] *Under the Quarry Woods* begins: 'Here, now'. There is something in this focus of childhood excitement, of Thomas Traherne's amazement in *Centuries of Meditation* at the appearance of the world. 'But being daily seen we observe it not', he says. Daily seeing, however, may have the opposite effect, and keep the amazement alive. I write in love of life, and because it passes. What I seek, and what I respond to in literary journals, is quickness: a word I first found in Henry Vaughan, and use to express the life of nature, but also a sense of the numinous. It bespeaks essential being, and one's emotional centre, or soul: that in the world and in oneself that intimates ultimate meaning.

---

[5] Ernest Hartley Coleridge, ed. *Animae Poetae* From the Unpublished Note-Books of Samuel Taylor Coleridge (London: William Heinemann, 1895), p. ix.
[6] *The Quotable Anaïs Nin* (San Antonio, Texas: Sky Blue Press, 2015), p. 81.
[7] Jeremy Hooker, *Welsh Journal* (Bridgend: Seren, 2001), p. 74

Under the Quarry Woods: journal into prose poetry

Animae Poetae was the well-chosen title of a selection from Coleridge's pocket books. These show the man in his world, revealing him body and soul. His self-consciousness brings to light the relational nature of the literary journal, the connection between inner and outer, mind and world, which he expressed beautifully in this way:

> In looking at objects of Nature while I am thinking, as at yonder moon dim-glimmering through the dewy window-pane, I seem rather to be seeking, as it were *asking* for, a symbolical language for something within me that already and for ever exists, than observing anything new.[8]

What this passage exemplifies is the interaction between mind and world, soul and nature, that characterises the literary journal. Thus, Dorothy Wordsworth has an acute eye for the life of nature, but what her journals also reveal is Dorothy herself. As with other writers in this tradition, the spirit of childhood animism lives on in her mature vision. At times, this rises to myth, as when she perceives the moon as female, thus feminizing the natural world she shared with her male companions. Francis Kilvert was another who, at moments of special intensity, would see the animate world in mythic terms, as when he says of some ancient oak trees: 'I fear those grey old men of Mocca'.[9]

For poets, there is a fine line between charged observation and poetry. As well as Coleridge, we may think of Gerard Manley Hopkins, for whom the very word 'charged', as in

---

[8] *Animae* Poetae, p. 136.
[9] David Lockwood, ed., *Kilvert, The Victorian, A New Selection from Kilvert's Diaries* (Bridgend: Seren Books, 1992), p. 274.

'God's Grandeur' ('The world is charged with the grandeur of God') informed his Christian vision, and shaped both his prose observations and his poems. For Hopkins instress was a felt mode of perception, a way of apprehending the identity of particular beings and things. The step from notebook to poem was a short one for Hopkins, in the sense that the alchemic process of transformation was already at work in the original charged observation. Something similar was true for Edward Thomas in his prose, as Robert Frost pointed out to him.

Like Edward Thomas as a boy, I found my principal literary influence in Richard Jefferies. Jefferies saw the life of nature intensely and his perception resulted in thinking that made him an iconoclast. He could not accept any explanation – any grand narrative – of the life he saw around him. Hence his espousal of what in 'Nature and Books' he called 'unlearning, the first step to learn', to 'coming to have touch of that which is real'. The process in Jefferies' writing is from sense experience – 'touch' of the real – to thought. He never stopped seeing and thinking for himself. Even near the end of his life he wrote in his notebook: 'I begin all again, striking out everything, fresh from the flower, the sun and the mind'. To the very last he is looking for himself, seeking to perceive the relationship between flower, sun, and mind: the meaning of life in the cosmos, which he called 'Sun Life'. Keywords here are 'fresh' and 'begin'.

'I begin all again', Jefferies says. Diary or journal, pocket book or daybook, whatever we call it, encourages this form of writing. Each day is a new day, offering a fresh start, with a freshness of expression. At the same time, it is a continuing process of sensing and thinking and seeking, of exploring.

As poet and critic, I have long thought of my work as exploratory. While this affirms independence, it also both acknowledges the magnitude of subject – whether another writer, or the life of nature – and the inevitable limitation and

Under the Quarry Woods: journal into prose poetry

partiality of my view. Exploration is a process; it is always on the way.

My journals or diaries have been the 'quarry' for my poems, as well as other writings. As a metaphor, quarry refers both to the whole journal and to the edited form.[10] In making each book, I had the help of my wife, Mieke's, keen eye in the editing process. In *Under the Quarry Woods* the editing and selecting was more severe, in order to 'cut' the prose poem from the material. Again, Mieke helped me to choose and arrange the passages. I had, too, the invaluable assistance of Liz Mathews, the publisher, who also provided visual images in harmony with the written contents.

Quarry, then, is a metaphor for the selecting and editing process. In this instance, it also refers specifically to subject, to a particular place. Some 18 years ago we bought a house beside a lane that goes up steeply to Treharris Park, on the edge of a former pit village. Among woods on the other side of the lane was a quarry which had been the source of stone for the Deep Navigation coalmine, sunk in the 1860s, and continuing to provide work until its closure on Good Friday 1991. This and other pits in the area had been what Zola in *Germinal* called the mine in Northern France: voracious. The area had witnessed terrible pit disasters, at Cilfynydd and Senghenydd, and the tragedy caused by the moving hill of slurry at Aberfan. The pits that had taken lives had also provided work that maintained a community and its way of life. And now Deep Navigation and the other pits had gone, to be replaced by parks and lakes, and a landscape of memory, and by unemployment.

---

[10] To date, I have published four edited journals: *Welsh Journal* (Seren, 2001), *Upstate: A North American Journal* (Shearsman Books, 2007), *Openings: A European Journal* (Shearsman Books, 2014), and *Diary of a Stroke* (Shearsman Books, 2016).

An emptiness and a question of meaning remained. This was where I found myself, literally a stranger in a foreign land.

The prose poems focus on the history and natural life of the area, on the memory of what made and unmade it, and on the question: what now? It is a social question, but it is personal too. *Under the Quarry Woods* asks where I am, and also what I am doing here, an English poet in this foreign place. The last question is mainly implicit. My focus is on the place itself.

Like the diary on which it draws, the prose poem sequence is a capacious form, capable of including voices other than the poet's. It is also able to move between the personal and the historical, and between the present moment and the past. Different voices entering the first passage on page 17 interrupt observation and meditation, asserting the claims of other lives:

> HANNAH LOVES ALEX written in black on the Cannons stone. Among love messages inked on the wooden bridge: I WOZ ERE, ERE I WOZ, WOZ I ERE YES I WOZ YEAH BOY!

Across the sequence other noises, as well as human voices – birds, traffic, wind, rain – are interrupted by an underlying silence, represented by the name of the village, Quakers Yard, visible from the quarry woods:

> Light flashes in my eyes from a window across the valley. I think of the Quakers laid in the ground by the bridge. Does the listening heart & mind leave a different silence?

A sense of aftermath associated with disasters underground weighs on the area:

Under the Quarry Woods: journal into prose poetry

> When he was a boy my friend walked over the mountain on a sunny morning in October one hundred years ago and saw this: great wheels above the colliery turning, taking the cages up and down the pit. When the wheels stopped, agony on the waiting faces, as the dead bodies were carried from the shaft. Rescuers made their wills before descending to where the roofs had fallen and fires raged. Today in the memorial garden boys and girls lay wreaths in remembrance of their great-grandfathers.

This passage refers to Walter Hadyn Davies, who was an old man when he befriended me during my early years in Wales. In his memoirs, he remembered the shock he received, as a boy, when having walked from his home over the mountain, he witnessed the immediate aftermath of the pit disaster at Senghenydd on 14 October 1913, in which 439 men and boys were killed.[11]

In *Under the Quarry Woods* the juxtaposition of passages represents an essential respect for life in its myriad human and natural forms. Eschewing the mastery of a single point of view, the sequence is a form of witness. It doesn't claim impersonality or detachment, and particular themes, concerns, and questions emerge insistently. Among these, the principal is power.

It is necessary now to quote a longer passage:

> Shadow falls across the page. In a violent blast the fir tree almost turns inside out.

---

[11] See Walter Haydn Davies, *Ups and downs* (Christopher Davies: Swansea, 1975), pp. 170 – 185.

A giant, ragged tower of cloud moves over, battlements shot through with light. It passes over, changing shape before I've found the words to describe it. I imagine a power that could blast us off the face of the earth.

Images form of powers that have driven through this country, changing its face, carrying or destroying or abandoning thousands of lives. One human intervention, one mechanism, like the railway and the possibilities it created, gives way to another, hurling humanity forward into another age. And to some the journey is beneficial; others think they know where they're going; and to some it's all blind fury, or emptiness.

We are not machines, however much they move us. It is always a human voice that we recognise.

Now the violence has increased. Wind-driven rain sweeps across the valley, shaking trees, blowing leaves against the window. Blown one way and another, leaves look as though they don't know whether to fly or fall. Telephone wires seem to stretch like elastic. Cloud ruins tumble behind the wind-ravaged fir. And for all that, houses in the valley look secure, though once a 'freak' tornado struck close by, demolishing buildings, and killing a man by blowing him against a wall. (UQW, p. 19)

'Images form': prose poetry like *Under the Quarry Woods* relies as much upon imagery as more traditional verse. Here, images are borne out of experience of the force of a storm in the outer

Under the Quarry Woods: journal into prose poetry

world. The natural power engenders imagination of 'a power that could blast us off the face of the earth'. This in turn leads to images of historical, mechanical power, together with reflections on its effect upon people's lives. The passage is not dissimilar to the more compact 'Matrix', as it makes a shape in words with sentences and paragraphs, and crystallizes in images, such as 'Cloud ruins tumble behind the wind-ravaged fir'. The piece is constructed to make a shape that corresponds to the storm. Its opening, 'Shadow falls across the page', announces the incursion of the outer world, and the storm that inspires the creation of metaphors and leads to reflection. The idea of mechanical power is overwhelming, and suggests 'blind fury, or emptiness'. What survives it is 'a human voice' and our ability to recognise one.

On other pages the juxtaposition of passages of different length reinforces the dynamic structure of the whole. Page 25 begins with a moment of personal nostalgia, caused by seagulls flying over a supermarket carpark:

> Distance returns, restless as the tides.
> My memory is salt with longing.

The following passages return to the life of the woods:

> Again the blown rain falls, running down & aslant the window. The fir tree shakes, and I can see trees shaking in the valley, above Quakers Yard. How many days of darkness this place has known, through lives I can only guess at.

> *

> Owls in the quarry woods on a still night, a featherweight of sound.

*

> A storm sky lies heavy on the hills. Light mist stands in the valley & in the woods. It is dark under the trees, the path a darkish red mixture of grit, stones, dead leaves. The stillness is deeper for barely perceptible movements – a water drop landing on a leaf, a twig released as a small bird flies off.

'Lives I can only guess at' exemplifies the spirit of unknowing that characterises *Under the Quarry Woods*, its refusal of a masterful overview or intimacy with other people's lives. One-line sections work like haiku. With its spacing of passages and images the sequence espouses a sort of Oriental poetics, which isolates particular beings and things against the background of cosmic space, represented by sky and cloud, and moon and sun. This plays against a distinctively Western historical consciousness and sense of time. Life inheres in the particular, in the moment that matters, such as a waterdrop landing on a leaf. Such movements underlie the depth of a metaphysical stillness and silence, represented by the movement of words against the whiteness of the page.

 Juxtaposed passages acknowledge the equality, the common significance, of creatures and things, conveying at once the value of the particular and the truth that all life is one. On page 27 there are four sections. The first, written after 'days of rain, welcomes 'a big half moon', 'like a visitor one hadn't expected to see again.' The second section focuses on 'a sleepy bumblebee' flying heavily close to the house wall, 'as if inspecting the paintwork or waiting to be let in'. In the next section, a walk in the park brings 'windflowers in the beech

Under the Quarry Woods: journal into prose poetry

woods' into view, and introduces the clashing sounds of jays and blackbirds. It concludes: 'Nothing fresher than the first two green leaves of an infant sycamore, just free of the soil'. Such natural freshness, in this area ravaged by history, is a recurring theme of the sequence. The fourth section crystallizes the significance of natural vision for human creativity:

> Grass blades shimmer with life, each defined, separately distinguishable, though growing together. Violets, wild strawberry flowers, nettles with white splashes of bird dung. For a poet or artist to 'make' anything corresponding to nature it's necessary to intimate the stream, the life flowing through the leaf.

Moon, bumblebee, infant sycamore, jays, blackbird, violets, strawberry flowers, nettles, grass blades: these are not random details, chosen for poetic effect; they are specific things or beings, belonging to what Wordsworth in *The Prelude* called 'this active universe': that which in poets such as Wordsworth and Blake, Coleridge and Ezra Pound, is the primary subject of poetry. Like the grass blades, each thing is both 'defined, separately distinguishable', and shimmering with life. These are not bits and pieces of natural phenomena, but manifestations of 'the stream' of life.

The final lines of the section are a poetic credo: 'For a poet or artist to 'make' anything corresponding to nature it's necessary to intimate the stream, the life flowing through the leaf'. This is what *Under the Quarry Woods* attempts as a 'made' thing, a shape in words. It is a work in which the poet places himself in the subject and gives priority to the matter, which is the nature and history of the quarry woods and surrounding area. The medium of prose poetry has something of the expansiveness of prose, but it carries within it the quickness that imagery of 'the stream of life' defines as the true subject of poetry.

To avoid misunderstanding, I should say at this point that not all my lyric poetry is quarried from my journal. From early on, I have been preoccupied as a poet with subject, more specifically, what I have come to call 'ground'. Often, I find that a lyric poem will begin with something as fugitive as a sense impression, such as rain in my face or the feel of shingle underfoot. It is, therefore, less a matter of beginning with prose and transforming it into poetry, and more of being enlivened by a kind of 'touch'. This animates the writing process and makes a way into the subject. It isn't something I wish to try to analyse. All I wish to say is that, with luck, it can happen independently, as well as through the journal. But the life of the journal has helped me to recognise quickness, which is what in my lyric poems I seek.

My work at the University of Glamorgan brought my wife and me, in 2001, to buy a house in Treharris, under the quarry woods. I had lived for some years in Ceredigion, but this part of Wales was new to me: an area of residual but fragmentary community once dependent upon the coal industry. The area had been newly landscaped, but still bore signs of former industrial uses. It was where a sense of identity was under pressure, as I knew from students from the Valleys of South Wales, young people with a family background of unemployment, uncertain about their future. I myself was a stranger, as my friend, the poet Anne Cluysenaar, pointed out to me, in a letter in which she generously responded to my poetry as a whole. Anne's personal history, as she acknowledged, meant that she couldn't identify with my original sense of a permanent 'home'. I had felt a strong sense of belonging to my native place in Hampshire between the New Forest and the Solent. *Under the Quarry Woods* marks the distance I had travelled from that:

Under the Quarry Woods: journal into prose poetry

I recall a sort of trance I would sometimes go into in class, when everything in and around me would become unreal, or change into a new dreamlike reality.

What then is strange?

Now, I would say it's the light of a common day: life as we wake into it, from the small self and the world it draws around it. Words have always come to me as provisional, a way of pointing at what is beyond them, at life with a strange identity that is not words.

The difference, here, is that my sense of belonging has lifted off, like mist blowing away from the hills. (*UQW*, p. 20)

While I go on to admit that the industrial history that has shaped the area was 'not my history', I acknowledge myself to be 'a product of the transformed world, the society made possible by coal and iron, the wealth of an empire, and what it left behind, which we barely understand'. The section concludes by affirming that strangeness is 'a realisation of connection', and 'not the idea alone, but the moment when one experiences it, shedding the self's insulation, the isolating carapace'.

I had always felt an outsider in Wales: it had been a way of respecting the otherness of Wales, as well as affirming my sense of English identity. *Under the Quarry Woods* interrogates the idea of strangeness to affirm an enlarged sense of common ground. The famous hymn speaks of being a stranger in a foreign land. This is my position as the speaker in *Under the*

Quarry Woods, where strangeness itself becomes a primary subject. It is the condition of a place that has been estranged from the purpose that made it, resulting in a sense of lostness experienced by people living there. Yet another idea of strangeness contrasts with ideas of isolation and alienation, and what *Under the Quarry Woods* ultimately affirms is a shared condition, in the strangeness of being alive.

Black faced ram
by Ann Lewis

JILL TOWNSEND

Waiting for Results

Pricked by growth
and unfamiliar warmth,
how cruel it is
to be in limbo.

Time tells the days
like inattentive prayers.
They have no answers
except themselves –

blue or grey skies,
a slip of snowdrop
heaving up through
stiff compost.

The everyday being
what I must hold,
not forecasts
or possibilities

while death is a smudge
on someone's thumb,
data, another
wet or fine work day.

My fear retreats
down their corridor
of boredom in search
perhaps of a reprieve.

Recovering

The sun's zest
falls like snowflakes.
A joyful awakening
to one with worries,
a shot of juice.

It catches on twigs
and the blind grass
as if everything
holds out its hands
to receive it

and as I look up
it touches my forehead
with a blessing –
fireball, crackling gas,
a shot to the head,

reduced by distance.
The sun receives pain
burning in the dark.
I am here still.
Enthralled. Overjoyed.

ROBERT NISBET

The Archaeologists

In the 1980s, some of the 16- and 17-year-old school leavers on the Government's Youth Training Scheme were asked to help on the archaeological dig at the Augustinian Priory site in the West Wales town of Haverfordwest.

> No navvies' pick and spade stuff here.
> They were asked just to dust a little,
> help, brush up, assist the assistants.
> So for eight hours a day, their quotidian,
> the football, pubs, street scuffle and banter,
> was subsumed slowly into history's dream.
>
> The Augustinians, their priory built
> by the wealth and politics of religion
> but surely in humility too, some gentleness,
> there, on the banks of the river, laid out
> their life, its stalls and refectories, retreats
> for prayer, its herb garden.
>
> Then came, in history's onward tramp,
> a busy port three hundred yards away,
> the sailors, brothels, alehouses,
> and then, the priory left now in neglect,
> the railway and industrial age.
>
> Then the coming of the archaeologists
> and the search for artefacts and atmosphere,
> for meditation's history.
>
> And the helpers, youths, the YTS boys,
> brushing, assisting the assistants?

Before the blooming of their futures,
the jobs and families and turbulence,
they brushed just momentarily
against a world of celibacy and thought,
of wonder and the spirit.

ANN PILLING

After the Funeral

After the funeral we walked on the headland
in un-fierce end of summer sun
where butterflies were

where caterpillars tigered black and gold
threaded the grass, where bees
found the last sea pinks unerringly, and fed.

Three heads in a line
a man and his daughters, faces
twisted like roots against grief.

The sea was a ridged silver, the blue air
scored white with wings. Friend of our life,
if this is all there is then it is beautiful,
the earth is beautiful, if this is all there is.

MARC HARSHMAN

Mariners

Two men sit talking, one voice with a whistle
    and the other a cough
    to mark their progress through the old stories.
Their shadows
    pool on the weed-clutched sidewalk
    below a paint-blistered bench.
Their necks are tilted,
    as if the weight of memory
    unbalanced their skulls.
And, perhaps, does – more deaths
    now than lives, with only these stories
    to raise those long gone
    above the shifting horizon.
And when their eyes meet to confirm
    the veracity
    in these ongoing resurrections,
      the tales they tell
      keep them afloat
        in that rearing ocean
          on this, their voyage out.

MARTIN POTTER

Walking the Old Beat

Turns a corner shambles
Along the pavement like
A distracted schoolchild
Back in the first terroir

Just those angles and measures revive
The deepest engraved geography
A virtual street palimpsest
Or a redecorated wall

With a persistent undercoat
Figures may come up through whitewash
And comfort of a delayed return
Resetting a nomadic dreamscape

Contemplate the Floor

Watch careless the window
Has spilt a puddle of light
Moving across the floor

A calibrated carpet
Could measure time leaving
No stain on the texture

Curling patterns' enigma
Floorboards' repetition
Illumined in succeeding

Patches of detached
Gestures towards sense
A hidden cloud draws over

RANAJIT SARKAR

The Bran-Tub

You can bring out many things
from the bran tub of
your infancy. Not everything
is matter for poetry.
Sometimes I grasp moments that
have no real shadow,
those are the hoardings I am most
fond of. I'll continue my
exploration in the bran
until my fingers seize
one day
my birth.

THOMAS R. SMITH

The Library of Heaven

When we find in the Library of Heaven
those volumes containing the poems
we meant to write but for some
reason didn't, our response will be
not regret but relief that they
somehow in Eternity got written
in spite of us or by a part of us
we didn't know was writing,
the very existence of which we had
only the faintest intuition,
and if someone else wrote them
instead of us it won't matter
because we will simply be
glad knowing they aren't lost,
loving them more than ourselves,
our ego won't be in it.

Palm Sunday

What a scene that must have been, people tearing
fronds off the palms, and their clothes too,
strewing them for the donkey to walk on,
animal of peace, not the horse of war
a king would ride in on. What sort of
king was this one who entered the city
astride such a mount? Fool-king, he clowned
his way through the Hosannas, acclaim rising
about him like the dust of a thousand
hooves, his own little army of love.
It was long ago, it was today,
it was in the heat, it was in the cold
of the northern spring, and people threw
down their clothes for the donkey's hooves to tread,
achieved nakedness in which to be seen
by him. It was noisy, it was hot,
the Emperor's swords and spears stayed while
the cries of revolution lifted him
  – and us – toward a life above the dust.

ALEX BARR

Iain

The tall tall slim French boy stood
in the rain with his back to me, his head
snug in a hood. I thought
for a moment it was Iain, my friend Iain
(two i's in his name) alive again.

In his attic we pulled out 78s and there
I first heard *When They Begin the Beguine*
that voluptuous tune. One voluptuous night
we played strip poker with the delicious nieces
of Mrs Lichfield. Very little flesh
got exposed. We chased them round the garden.

In his cellar and my washhouse
we messed with flowers of sulphur,
zinc, permanganate,
and hydrochloric acid, and he told me
Norma, whom we met on the cricket field
and whom I ached for, really liked me.
It was a lie.

Late one afternoon
making our way to Scout camp after a hike
(it seems we'd lost the rest of our patrol)
he enforced a three-mile detour
along a country lane. I counted telegraph poles
to counter weariness. When I complained he said,
with the authority of his extra year,
'Scouts do things the hard way.'

In Barr's Private Army
(we were eleven) he was made a lance-jack
but later in the Queen's Own Khaki Squaddies
only a private. Nonetheless he claimed,
'I'm dating the Colonel's daughter.'

Was *that* a lie? I see him saying it,
hair butchered by the regimental barber,
tall, horse-faced, outside the Jolly Sailor
with great aplomb. On that same spot
I learned that he had died at forty-two.

The French boy turned, and oh, he wasn't Iain

KENNETH STEVEN

Finally

That's what you said: that often at the end
when we've begun to drift away, to float
between the dark of death and some far distant light,
we come back for a moment, waken wide
to tell of those we've met and spoken with
almost as if we'd really seen them, been with them –
the ones that go a long way back, but that instead
we're hearing voices from the other side
and do not understand that's where they are –
talking, calling, beckoning – as if to pull
us from the no man's land that lies between;
and try to meet us, bring us safely back
to where we once began, that promised land
we dared to dream would be the place we found.

At Pluscarden Abbey

Only once have I stood beneath a tree
holding my breath to hear an owl.
Its voice was ragged; tattered at the edges –
a call that carried wide across the woods
in the still blue warmth that August dusk.
And everywhere along the valley's edge
came callings of other owls until I thought
they talked to one another, voices
almost like strange lamps strung out into the night
over a darkened sea.
I held my breath and heard their woven calls
as the moon rose whole and huge above the
hills.

BEATRICE TEISSIER

Jacques at the Solstice

The night you died

      the tipping point

took its time

                but the tilt was

    where you wanted it:

                towards the light.

Cremation Day

I had not wanted
    to think of ashes
        and went walking
by the sea,
    found a gull:

wings frayed,
    innards out,
        eyes gone,

        'the tide will take it'
                said a man;
    then the beak
             blue-lined, dense, sharp
        cried:
            'death is out of my grasp.'

Signal

The morning after the bomb,
floor, three walls and staircase gone,

memory swims for the hot lived space,

finds no limits,
fixes on paper snapping
in the wind on the one wall

like a broken sail
calling out its release.

HUBERT MOORE

Back-licking

I'm watching an ordinary
grey cow that needs its back
if not scratching, licking.
Maybe all cows have necks
so multi-jointed they can turn
and lick themselves on the back.
I'm not into licking but I need
to swivel quietly round
and catch myself and what's
in the field behind me
unaware: legs folded under it,
head thrust (if cows were us)
mournfully, beautiful grey cow.

DENNI TURP

System Incompatibility

Relentless winds and weeks of rain
have trashed this garden, wounded earth
and branch alike, left ruin in their wake.
Mud gluts paths and branches litter
winter's grief across the grass.
I replace the lid torn from the water butt,
secure the gale-loosed gate, then stand and wait.

In the starkness of the hawthorn hedge
a robin flickers by the lane and calls.
Jackdaws pass overhead in single file.
It's getting late, the sun bleeds low,
and fairy rings of far too early daffodils
crowd in hopeful clusters beneath the trees.
Red tips of Glossy Abelia glow match head buds
to spark the day, and the first pale primrose of the year
tries to shine a yellow flourish for the coming spring.

In fields beyond the walls, sparrows set down stones
in pictograms that we've forgotten how to read,
crows scrutinise the ground for signs
beneath where buzzards wheel the skies,
and as the light retreats, moles dig and pile
to spell out earth mound sentences we fail
to understand or even recognise.

CHRISTINE VALTERS PAINTNER

Beloved

Your body a cluster of grapes,
sweet, filled with promise of wine
your lips pour moonlight

across open fields,
your hands, maps to secret
universes, lead me to treasure,

your eyes an invitation
to quiet forests
your back, stone face, a cliff rising,

your teeth, a row of white houses
saying welcome.
I love all of you: thigh, tongue, torso,

hold nothing back from me beloved
your love a river where salmon
swim strong, determined.

One day the earth will claim us again,
take us back into its soft ground
for now, hold me with your eager arms

as we count the hours,
each a globe of light,
calling each one gift.

Henry Vaughan, Scholarly Editor

DONALD R. DICKSON

While Henry Vaughan's reputation as poet and medical practitioner is secure, his work as a scholarly editor has not been given its full due. Those who knew him certainly regarded his learning highly. In his preface to *Thalia Rediviva* (1678), John Williams, then a prebendary of St David's Cathedral, asserted that Vaughan's friends '*know him very well able to give himself a lasting Monument, by undertaking any Argument of note in the whole Circle of Learning*' and several of the dedicatory poems address him as 'learned.'[1] To redress this deficiency I would like to examine the marginal notes and other annotations added to both his prose translations and original compositions to better appreciate his considerable erudition and critical discernment: in a word, his editorial acumen. I shall begin with his 'Advertisement' to Eucherius's *De contemptu mundi epistola parænetica ad Valerianum* in the second part of *Flores Solitudinis* (1654), which introduces *The World Contemned* with both textual history and biographical detail and offers an overview of Vaughan's methods. Then I will review the many annotations added to his prose works, in which he draws on his wide knowledge of classical poetry (such as Juvenal, Horace, Seneca, Lucan, and so forth) as well as of contemporary poets, such as Petrarch or Baudouin Cabilliau, to illuminate passages for his readers. In similar fashion he adds numerous clarifying notes of an historical nature. Finally, I will raise and try to answer an intriguing question: where could he

---

[1] All references are to *The Works of Henry Vaughan*, ed. Donald R. Dickson, Alan Rudrum, and Robert Wilcher, 3 vols. (Oxford: Oxford University Press, 2018), 723. See, e.g., Thomas Powell's 'Upon the Ingenious Poems of his Learned Friend, Mr. Henry Vaughan the Silurist' in *Works*, 725.

have gotten access to such texts in rural Wales in the middle of a Civil War?

The preface to one of the works Vaughan translated in his 1654 *Flores Solitudinis* illustrates his editorial acumen quite well. *Flores* is printed in two sections, each with separate title pages and pagination. The first section contains two treatises by a Jesuit contemporary, Juan Eusebio Nieremberg y Otin (1595-1658); the second contains *The World Contemned* by the fifth-century churchman, St. Eucherius of Lyon, and the biography of another early Christian saint, Paulinus of Nola, both translated from texts edited by the hagiographer Héribert Rosweyde (1569-1629), professor of philosophy in the Jesuit college at Douai.[2] *The World Contemned* is an epistolary essay written by Eucherius (*c.*380-449), a Roman citizen who gave up his life of wealth and privilege to live in the monastery of Lérins on a small island off Antibes following the death of his wife. His *De contemptu mundi* is an exhortation to his kinsman Valerian to show contempt for the world while still living in it. Here is Vaughan's 'Advertisement' or preface to his readers:

Advertisement.

Heribert Ros-weyd *published this peece at* Antwerp 1621. *It is mentioned by* Gennadius cap. 63. De Scriptoribus Ecclesiasticis; *and* Erasmus (*long before* Ros-weyd's *Edition) writ some Notes upon it. The Author* Euchcrius *was a* Roman *Senatour, but being converted to the Faith, he left the* Senate, *and lived in a poor* Cell

---

[2] D. Eucherii, Episcopi Lugdunensis de contemptu mundi: Epistola parænetica ad Valerianum cognatum. Accedit vita D. Paulini Nolani veri mundi contemptoris, ed. Héribert Rosweyde (Antwerp, 1621), abbreviated DCM.

by the river Druentium, *where his Wife* Galla *died. His two daughters,* Consortia, *and* Tullia, *having learnt* Christ, *continued both in the Virgin-life,* & signorum gloriâ claruerunt. *He sate Bishop in the chair of* Lyons *(as I find him placed by* Helvicus) *in the year of our Lord* 443. *Some will have him a Century lower, but that difference weakens not the certainty of it. The peece it self (in the Original) is most elaborate and judicious, and breaths that* togatam elegantiam *which in most of the* Roman *Senatours was not more acquired, then natural. What this* Valerian *was (more then our Authors Kinsman, by whose pen his name lives) is not certainly known. Some will have him to be* Priscus Valerianus, *the Præfect, or Deputy of* France, *mentioned by* Sidonius Apollinaris: *Others are willing to let him passe for that* Valerian, *whose* Homilies *now extant were published by* Sirmondus. *But as it is not determinable, so is it not material: This we may safely conclude, that he was a very eminent, noble* Personage, *and one that followed too much after temporal* pomp, *and the* powers *of this* world; *though neither of them could lend him so much light, as would keep him from* obscuritie. *To bring down these top-branches,* Eucherius *layes the* Axe *to the root of the tree, by shewing him the* vanity, *and the* iniquity *of* riches *and* honours, *the two grand inticements of* popular spirits. *And this he doth with such powerfull and clear reasons, that to virtuous and peaceful minds he hath renderd them not only* contemptible, *but* odious. *Much more might have been spoken against them, but (seeing the Age we live in hath made all his* Arguments, Demonstrations) *he hath in my judgement spoken enough.*

H. V. S.

As he always does with his translations, Vaughan begins by indicating his source, an edition by the prolific Jesuit Rosweyde (whose other works he would make use of elsewhere), while referring also to an earlier edition with notes by Erasmus; he then establishes the authenticity of the text with the *Bibliotheca Ecclesiastica* of the church historian Gennadius of Massilia.[3] Some biographical details are added from Rosweyde's 'Vitæ S. Evcherii Brevicvlvm' (whose source is the *Martyrologium* of Ado of Vienne), including the tribute to his daughters: *signorum gloriâ claruerunt* ('they were illuminated by the glory of their miracles').[4] Going beyond the simple biography found in his source text, Vaughan dates Eucherius's bishopric in 443 using the German historian Christoph Helwig[5] and also muses over the identity of the dedicatee Priscus Valerianus (*fl.* 450–6), praetorian prefect of Gaul and a cousin of Eucherius. Vaughan

---

[3] D. *Eucherii, Episcopi Lugdunensis De contemptu mundi: Epistola parænetica ad Valerianum cognatum. Accedit vita D. Paulini Nolani veri mundi contemptoris*, ed. Héribert Rosweyde (Antwerp, 1621), abbreviated *DCM*. Erasmus published his edition *Evcherii formvlarvm intelligentiæ spiritualis Liber* (Basil, 1530), with the scholia, 129–31. An edition of *Bibliotheca ecclesiastica, sive nomenclatores VII. veteres* was published in Antwerp, (1646) that Vaughan could have seen.
[4] *DCM*, sigs. *10ᵛ-*12ʳ.
[5] Christoph Helwig (or Helvig, 1581–1617), historian and professor of Hebrew and Greek at the University of Gießen; see *Theatrvm historicvm et chronologicvm æqualibus denariorum, quinquagenariorum & centenariorum intervallis* (5th edn. Oxford, 1651), 100, which places 'EVCHERIVS *Lugdunensis episcopam in Gallia*' in the year 443.

knows that Sidonius Apollinaris (c.430–89), Gallo-Roman from Lyon, sent Priscus Valerianus a selection of his verses and praised him as a critic.[6] He also recognizes another possibility in St. Valerianus, bishop of Cimiez near Nice (fl. 439–55), whose homilies were edited by Jacques Sirmond, one of the greatest scholars of the seventeenth century.[7] In this brief preface, then, is much learning, which is also evident throughout his original prose, his translations, and his paratexts as he adds clarifying details from classical, patristic, and contemporary sources to enrich his works.

Classical Sources

Vaughan glosses his translations or adds illustrations to his own prose from a number of classical authors, especially his favorite Juvenal whose 'tenth Satyre' is translated in his first volume of verse. For example in *Olor Iscanus* he glosses Plutarch's description of Pompey as 'effeminate' – who is careful not to disorder his hair styling by using only one finger to scratch his head – by noting:

> *This was held by the Romans for a sure mark of lasciviousnes. Iuvenal toucheth upon't.* – huc venient carpento, et navibus omnes | Qui digito scalpunt uno Caput. –

The observation is from *Satire* IX.131–33: in the Loeb translation, 'from every quarter, in carriages and in ships, those

---

[6] See 'Carmen VIII' ('Ad Priscvm Valerianvm Virvm Praefectorivm') in Sidonius, *Poems and Letters*, tr. W. B. Anderson, 2 vols. (Loeb Classical Library, 1936, 1965), I, 170–1.
[7] The edition to which Vaughan refers is *Sancti Valeriani episcopi Cemeliensis homiliae XX*, ed. Jacques Sirmond (Paris, 1612).

gentry who scratch their heads with one finger will flock in.'[8] In his own *Man in Darkness*, he expatiates on the *ubi sunt* trope in a marginal gloss from Juvenal's *Satire* X.172-73: 'mors sola fatetur | Quantula sunt hominum corpuscula', which may be translated as 'Death alone proclaims how small are our poor human bodies!'[9] Lastly in *Of Temperance and Patience* he explains the infamous punishment for parricides known as the *Sack* or *poena cullei*.

> *Pliny mentions this punishment: the parricide after his apprehension, to augment the horror of his conscience, was first whipt with rods dipt in the blood of his murthered parents: and afterwards together with a dog, an ape, and a cock, (Creatures which shew little reverence towards their sires) he was thrust alive into a strong sack, and so thrown into the Sea.*[10]

Pliny actually does not mention the *poena cullei*; Juvenal, however, does in *Satire* VIII, 214.[11] The lurid details of this description may have been impressed upon him during his days

---

[8] *Works*, 240. For the translation, see *Juvenal and Persius*, tr. G. G. Ramsay (Loeb Classical Library, 1918; rev. 1940), 190–91.
[9] *Works*, 318. For the translation, see *Juvenal and Persius*, 206–07. For another use in *Man in Darkness* of Juvenal, *Satire* XIII, 86-88, see *Works*, 323.
[10] *Works*, 406.
[11] See *Juvenal and Persius*, 174–75: 'cuius supplicio non debuit una parari | simia nec serpens unus nec culleus unus' [for whose chastisement no single ape or adder, no solitary sack, should have been provided].

at the Inns of Court. There are otherglosses to Horace,[12] to Seneca,[13] to Lucan,[14] to Plautus,[15] and to Petronius Arbiter.[16] He incorporates a line from the *Astronomicon*, a didactic poem on celestial phenomenon by the Roman poet Marcus Manilius: 'Sic nostros casus solatur mundus in astris.'[17] Vaughan adds an anecdote (i.e., one not given by Nieremberg) about '*One of the Indian Gymnosophists*' who immolated himself in the presence of Alexander the Great taken from a lesser known work, Arrian's *Anabasis of Alexander*,[18] and offers a note on the '*inhabitants of Pelusium*' that probably derives from Ammianus Marcellinus.[19] Likewise an apothegm from Sir Walter Raleigh's *Historie of the World* is glossed with a quotation from *De doctorum indagine* by the Roman grammarian Nonius Marcellus (*fl.* Early fourth century).[20]

---

[12] Horace, *Epistle* I.iv.13, in *Works*, 331; *Odes*, 4.7.7–12, in *Works*, 332; *Odes*, 4.9.25–28, in *Works*, 427; and *Odes*, 1.12.45–46, in *Works*, 489.

[13] Seneca, *Phoenissæ*, 197–98 (*Tragedies*, tr. Frank Justus Miller, 2 vols. [Loeb Classical Library, 1953], II, 358–59), in *Works*, 315; *Agamemnon*, 607–10 (*Tragedies*, II, 50–53) in *Works*, 316; *Hippolitus*, 162–64 (*Tragedies*, I, 330–31), in *Works*, 326; and *Thyestes*, 449–51 (*Tragedies*, II, 128–29), in *Works*, 329.

[14] Lucan, *Pharsalia, The Civil War*, tr. J. D. Duff (Loeb Classical Library, 1928, VII.819; in *Works*, 329.

[15] An epigraph to *Hermetical Physick* is taken from the spurious prologue to Plautus's *Pseudolus*, 3–6, in *Works*, 645. Though not printed in modern editions, such as the Loeb, this prologue was often printed in Vaughan's time.

[16] Petronius Arbiter, *Satyricon*, tr, Michael Heseltine (Loeb Classical Library, 1912), 119.33–38, in *Works*, 317.

[17] Manilius, *Astronomicon*, ed. A. E. Housman, 5 vols. (Cambridge: Cambridge University Press, 1937), II, 261, in *Works*, 322.

[18] Arrian, *Anabasis of Alexander*, tr. E. Iliff Robson, 2 vols. (Loeb Classical Library, 1947), VII.iii.1–6, in *Works*, 430.

[19] Ammianus Marcellinus, *Roman History*, tr. John C. Rolfe, 3 vols. (Loeb Classical Library, 1935), XXII.16.3 (II, 297), in *Works*, 407.

[20] *De doctorum indagine*, XII.30-2, in *De compendiosa doctrina*, ed. L. Quicherat (Paris, 1872), 615; in *Works*, 316: 'N. Marcellus de

Lastly, Vaughan tries to remedy an uncertain reference to *Callistratus* made by Nieremberg with a marginal note that identifies him as '*One of the Counsellors of* Alexand. *The great.*'[21] Probably meant is the historian Callisthenes of Olynthus (*c.*370-27 BC), who accompanied Alexander during his campaigns to record the *Deeds of Alexander*, which does not survive.

Patristic Sources

Vaughan adds glosses to his own compositions from a variety of patristic sources. In the prayer he offers before taking communion in *The Mount of Olives*, he petitions 'that I may suck salvation from thy heart, that spring of the blood of God, which flowes into all believers', which he annotates with words from *De cœna Domini*.[22] This tract, attributed to St. Cyprian, enjoyed wide circulation in the Middle Ages and was available

---

doctorum indagine. Potest fatum morum mutabilitate converti, ut ex iis celerius vel tardius aut bonum fiat, aut pessimum.' The Latin may be translated: 'the fate of customs can be so altered by fickleness, that from them, sooner or later, either a good or very bad thing may happen.'

[21] *Works*, 446. Nieremberg, *De arte voluntatis*, rev. ed. (Lyon, 1649), referred to hereafter as *DAV*, 555–6, writes: 'Callistratus libro quastionum primo, legato honorari dixit. Suffragium, iudiciúmque morentium captabant, iam mortis vicinia sapientium, venerandorum.' This would seem to refer to Callistratus the Roman jurist (*fl.* in the reign of Septimius Severus, BC 198–211), who wrote two books of *Questiones* that survive only in Justinian's *Digest*. This quotation, however, does not appear in the *Digest*, nor is it among the quotations from Callistratus's *Qvaestionum Liber I* in Karl Hommel's compendium, *Palingenesia librorvm ivris␣␣␣␣␣vetervm sive Pandectarvm loca integra*, 3 vols. (Leipzig, 1767–8), I, 143.

[22] *Works*, 309: '*Cyprian* de cænâ domini. Cruci hæremus, sanguinem fugimus, & inter ipsa redemptoris nostri vulnera figimus linguam' [We cling to the cross, we flee his blood, and we affix our tongue to the wounds themselves of our redeemer].

in various editions and collections such as Andreas Spanner, *Polyanthea sacra ex universae sacrae Scripturae* (1615).[23] In *Man in Darkness* he cites a quip made famous by the desert anchorite St. Hilarion (d. 371): '*Go forth, O my soul, go forth; what is it that thou art afraid of ? Seventy yeers almost hast thou serv'd Christ, and art thou now afraid of death?*' In a marginal note he gives lines in Latin from the St. Jerome's *Vita Hilarionis*, which he may have found in one of his favorite sources, Rosweyde's *Vitæ patrum* (Antwerp, 1628):

> Egredere, quid times? Egredere anima mea;
> Septuaginta propè annis Christo servisti, &
> mortem times? *Hieron*. In vitâ *Hilar*.[24]

Jerome wrote the life of Hilarion in 390 at Bethlehem with the object of promoting the ascetic life, so it may be more legend than genuine history. Another patristic source that Vaughan treasures is St. Anselm (1033–1109), the Benedictine monk and theologian who is considered the founder of Scholasticism. Vaughan translates his *De felicitate sanctorvm* as *Man in Glory*.[25] Its topic is the state of the soul and body after death.

---

[23] See Spanner, *Polyanthea sacra ex universae sacrae Scripturae*, 3 vols. (Venice, 1709), I, 322; an earlier edition (Augsburg, 1615), could have been seen by Vaughan. In the edition available in the Hereford Cathedral Library, *D. Caecilii Cypriani Carthaginiensis episcopi, et gloriosissimi martyris opera* (Geneva, 1593), the reference to *De cœna Domini* is on page 502. The Cwm library also had a copy of St. Cyprian's *Opera* (Cologne, 1617), which is in Hereford today.

[24] *Works*, 319. See *Vitæ patrum: de vita et verbis seniorum libri X. Historiam, eremiticam complectentes*, ed. Héribert Rosweyde, 2nd ed. (Antwerp, 1628), 85. In *Man in Darkness*, *Works*, 329, he also refers to the story of the crow who brings bread to the hermit, St. Hilarion from St. Jerome's *Vita S. Pauli primi eremitæ*, in *Patrologia Latina*, XXIII, cols. 25–6.

[25] *S. Anselmi de felicitate sanctorvm dissertatio, exscriptore Eadinero*, ed. Jean-Baptiste de Machault, S.J. (Paris, 1639).

In his preface to the reader, Vaughan highlights those facets of the life story of St. Anselm that made him so relevant to the present age:

> Anselmus Archbishop of *Cantorbury* lived here in *Britaine*, in the reigne of *Rufus*, and striving to keep entire the Immunities of the Church, (which the spirit of Covetousnesse and Sacriledge did then begin to encroach upon,) he was twice banished.[26]

Oppressed by political leaders and forced into retirement, yet finding solace in thoughts of heavenly life, Anselm is clearly a beacon in troubled times of the 1650s.[27] Vaughan also interpolates a passage into the life of Paulinus from St. Augustine's *Confessions* whose author is identified in the margin.[28]

Contemporary Sources

In his own *memento mori* composition, *Man in Darkness*, Vaughan makes use of his wide reading in contemporary

---

[26] *Works*, 338.

[27] Vaughan also glosses a theological note countering a claim made by Anselm, *Works*, 348: 'This is onely proposed, not asserted, nor (indeed) can it be, for our Saviour himself tels us, That there is joy in the presence of the Angels of God over one sinner that repenteth, *Luke* 15.10. and their song is, *good will towards men*.'

[28] *Works*, 473: 'quid est hoc, quod audisti? surgunt indocti et caelum rapiunt, et nos cum doctrinis nostris ecce ubi volutamur in carne et sanguine!' From Augustine, *Confessions*, tr. William Watts, 2 vols. (Loeb Classical Library, 1912), VIII.viii (I, 443).

authors. To link the deplorable conditions that followed the Puritan occupation of Wales to the millenarianism of his age – as he says, 'we have seen his Ministers cast out of the Sanctuary, & barbarous persons without *light* or *perfection*, usurping holy offices' – Vaughan calls attention to a specific source in a marginal note:

> There is extant a little book called *Speculum Visionis* printed at *Norimberge* 1508, wherein this fearful desolation and destruction of the Church by Lay-men is expressely foretold.[29]

Vaughan refers to Joseph Grünpeck's pamphlet, *Speculum naturalis cœlestis & propheticæ visionis: omnium calamitatum tribulationum & anxietatum: quæ super omnes status: stirpes & nationes christianæ reipublice: presertim quæ cancro & septimo climati subiecte sunt: proximis temporibus venture sunt* (Nuremberg, 1508). A physician and astrologer, Grünpeck (*c.*1473–1532) argued that prophecy was influenced by the cycles of sun, moon, and planets.[30] There are also several glosses from the encyclopedia of Raffaelo Maffei, such as his explanation that Sybaris is '*A towne in the higher* Calabria *in* Italy 20. *Miles distant from* Rome', or his biographical note on Eustathius.[31] Moreover, in his biography of Paulinus, Vaughan adds a long, historically accurate note that is not drawn from

---

[29] *Works*, 316.
[30] Grünpeck's works were placed on the Index because of his interest in the occult sciences. On the millenarianism of the age, see Brian W. Ball's classic study, *A Great Expectation: Eschatological Thought in English Protestantism to 1660* (Leiden: Brill, 1975).
[31] Raffaelo Volaterranus, *Commentariorvm vrbanorvm Raphaelis Volaterrani, octo et triginta libri* (Basel, 1559), 140, in *Works*, 386; and *Commentariorvm vrbanorvm*, 356–57, in *Works*, 388.

his source and thus is the product of his own scholarship: '*This was about the year of our L. 428 about which time the Vandals after their excursions through* Polonia, Italy, Franconia, *and* Andalusia *had setled in* Africk....'[32] Vaughan refers to the battle of Ad Decimum near Carthage on 13 September 533, when the Roman army of the eastern empire under Belisarius defeated the Vandal forces of Gelimer.

As might be expected of a poet fond of Latin verse, Vaughan made use of contemporary poets he was reading, notably Petrarch from whose *De otio religiosorum*, *Africa*, and *De contemptu mundi* he quotes.[33] He also was familiar with Jesuit writers such Baudouin Cabilliau (1568–1652) whose epigram he used to show that the torpedo fish had the power to stop ships like the winter winds of Abydos, quickly killing in its frigid chains:

> Arcanas hyemes & cæca papavera ponti
> Abdo sinu, & celerem frigida vincla necem.[34]

Or the Bavarian Jesuit Johannes Bissel (1601–82) whose satirical novel *Icaria* details humorously his flight from the Swedes in the Thirty Years' War to show the vanity of earthly endeavors.[35] He quotes a proverb, '*the night is the mother of*

---

[32] *Works*, 522.
[33] *De otio religiosorum*, Liber II, in *Opera omnia*, 4 vols. in 1 (Basel, 1554), 355, in *Works*, 317; *Africa*, II.431, II.464–65, in *Opera omnia*, 367, in *Works*, 329; *De contemptu mundi*, Dialogvs III, in *Opera omnia*, 414–15, in *Works*, 332; and *De contemptu mundi* in *Opera omnia*, 367, in *Works*, 329.
[34] Baudouin Cabilliau, *Epigrammata selecta* (Antwerp, 1620), 7, in *Works*, 331.
[35] Johannes Bissel, *Icaria* (Ingolstadt, 1637), 215–16, in *Works*, 369.

thoughts', for which he gives the Italian in the margin.[36] He translates a long passage from the Neo-Latin writer Giovanni Aurelio Augurello (1441–1524), the alchemist known for his allegorical poem on making gold, *Chrysopoeia*, who wrote also consoling Pietro Lippomano (1504–48), bishop of Bergamo and of Verona, on the death of his sister.

> Peter, *when thou this pleasant world dost see,*
> *Beleeve, thou seest meere* Dreames *and* vanitie;
> *Not* reall *things, but* false: *and through the* Aire
> *Each where, an empty, slipp'rie* Scene, *though faire.*
> *The chirping* birds, *the fresh* woods *shadie boughes,*
> *The* leaves *shrill whispers, when the* west-wind *blowes.*
> *The swift, fierce* Greyhounds *coursing on the plaines,*
> *The flying* hare *distrest 'twixt feare and paines*;
> *The bloomy* Mayd *decking with* flowers *her head,*
> *The gladsome, easie* youth *by light* love *lead;*
> *And whatsoe'r heere with admiring eyes*
> *Thou seem'st to see, 'tis but a fraile disguise*
> *Worne by* eternall things, *a passive* dresse
> *Put on by* beings *that are passiveles.*[37]

Vaughan likewise adds a marginal gloss on the vanity of '*humane delights*' by creating a cento from several authors:

> Non est, falleris, hæc beata non est,
> Quam vos creditis esse, vita non est.

---

[36] *Works*, 314: 'A Proverb in *Italy*, La notte é madre de pensieri.' See Giovanni Torriano, *Select Italian Proverbs* (London, 1649), 67, identified first by Louise Guiney, *The Mount of Olives* (London: Henry Frowde, 1902), 43, n. 2.

[37] 'Ad Petrum Lipomanum in Obitu Claræ Sororis', ll. 1–14 from *Geronticon* (Antwerp, 1582), 92, in *Works*, 370:

> Fulgentes manibus videre gemmas,
> Aut auro bibere, & cubare cocco:
>
> Qui vultus Acherontis atri,
> Qui Styga tristem non tristis videt,
> Audétque vitæ ponere finem,
> Par ille regi, par superis erit.[38]

The first four lines are from a poem that Vaughan may have encountered in Joseph Justus Scaliger's *Catalecta veterum poetarum* that was first published as an appendix to an edition of Virgil, where it was one 'Item' among many under the heading 'De Vita Tranqvilla'; other editors attributed these lines to the 'De vita beata' of Pentadius (*fl.* 354–61), to Petronius Arbiter, or to Seneca.[39] The Latin may be translated: 'This is not, you are mistaken, the happy life which you believe it to be: to see gems shining on your hands, or to drink out of golden vessels and to recline in scarlet garments.' The last four lines are from Seneca's *Agamemnon*: 'who on the face of dark Acheron, on fearful Styx can look, unfearful, and is bold enough to put an end to life. A match for kings, a match for the high gods will he be.'[40] In *Man in Darkness* he also quotes from an epic poem in twelve books on the signs of the zodiac by Pier Angelo Manzolli or Marcellus Palingenius (*c*.1500–c.1543), whom he later celebrated in his poem, 'In Zodiacum Marcelli

---

[38] *Works*, 316.
[39] *Publii Virgilii Maronis Appendix cum supplemento multorum antehac nunquam excusorum poematum veterum poetarum* (Leiden, 1573), 197–98 (lines 1–3, 6).
[40] Seneca, *Agamemnon*, 607–10, in *Tragedies*, II, 50–53.

Palingenii';[41] he also alludes to one of Herbert's *Outlandish Proverbs*.[42] So his translations and original compositions are studded with passages from classical, patristic, and contemporary authors that explain or amplify the argument as Renaissance texts so often do through *copia*.

Private Libraries

A considerable body of research, thus, lies behind the glosses and commentary that augment his prose. Vaughan needed the following books (not including the major classical poets whose works would have been the easiest to acquire):

Ammianus Marcellinus. *Roman History* (many editions available)

Anselm, St. *De felicitate sanctorvm*, ed. Jean-Baptiste de Machault. Paris 1639. 8°.

Augurello, Aurelio. *Geronticon*. Antwerp, 1582. 8°.

Bisselius, Johannes. *Icaria*. Ingolstadt, 1637. 24°.

Bolton, Robert. *Last and Learned Worke of the Foure last Things*. London, 1632. 8°.

Bucholtzer, Abraham. *Index chronologicus* (many editions available). 2°.

---

[41] Marcellus Palingenius, *Zodiacus vitæ* (London, 1602), IX.180–1, XI.658–60, and VIII.249–51 (190, 254, and 164), in *Works*, 322. For Vaughan's 'In Zodiacum Marcelli Palingenii', see *Works*, 737.

[42] Herbert's *Outlandish Proverbs*, no. 942, in *The Works of George Herbert*, ed. F. E. Hutchinson (Oxford: Clarendon Press, 1941), 352, in *Works*, 328.

Cabilliau, Baudouin. *Epigrammata selecta*. Antwerp, 1620. 12°.

Cyprian, St. *De cænâ domini* (many editions available). 2°.

Eucherius, St. *De Contemptu Mundi*, ed. Héribert Rosweyde. Antwerp, 1621. 12°.

Eucherius, St. *Epistola parænetica . . . cum scholijs Erasmi Roterodami*. Bascl, 1530. 8°.

Ferrari, Giovanni Baptista. *Flora, sive De florvm cvltvra libri IV*. Rome, 1633. 8°.

Gennadius. *De Scriptoribus Ecclesiasticis* (many editions available).

Grünpeck, Joseph. *Speculum naturalis cœlestis & propheticæ visionis*. Nuremberg, 1508. 2°

Helwig, Christoph. *Theatrvm historicvm* (many editions available). 2°.

Jerome, St. *Vita Hilarionis* (many editions of his *Opera* available).

Jerome, St. *Vita S. Pauli primi eremitæ* (many editions of his *Opera* available).

Jerome, St. *Vitae sanctorum patrum* (many editions available).

Maffei, Raffaelo. *Commentariorvm vrbanorum ... Volaterrani* (1544, 1552, 1559). 2°.

Manilius, Marcus. *Astronomicon* (many editions available).

Manzolli, Pier Angelo. *Zodiacus vitæ* (many editions available).

Marcellus, Nonius. *De doctorum indagine* (many editions available).

Matthieu, Pierre. *Vnhappy Prosperity*. London, 1639. 4°.

Myle, Ægidius van der. *Oblectatio vitæ rusticæ*. Stettin, 1633. 12°.

Nieremberg, Juan Eusebio. *De arte voluntatis*. Lyon, 1631; Paris, 1639; Lyon, 1649. 8°.

Nolle, Heinrich. *Systema medicinæ hermeticæ generale*. Frankfurt, 1613. 8°.

Paulinus, St. *Divi Paulini episcopi Nolani opera*, ed. H. Rosweyde. Antwerp, 1622. 8°.

Petrarca, Francesco. *De contemptu mundi* (many editions of his **Opera** available). 2°.

Rainolds, John, tr. *Orationes duodecim*. Oxford, 1614, 1619, 1628. 12°.

Scaliger, Joseph Justus. *Catalecta veterum poetarum*. Leiden, 1573. 8°.

Sirmond, Jacques. *Sancti Valeriani episcopi Cemeliensis homiliæ XX*. Paris, 1612. 12°.

Torriano, Giovanni. *Select Italian Proverbs*. London, 1649. 12°.

Where Vaughan gained access to the many books necessary for this research is an enigma. Initially we might suspect that he had access to a 'gentry library', as John Donne, for example, is thought to have used the library of Henry Percy, ninth Earl of Northumberland, to do research for *Ignatius His Conclave* (1611).[43] While this is plausible, it is not very likely. Of the more than thirty books he unquestionably used (leaving aside the commonplace Greek or Latin poets), fewer than half are even listed in the Private Libraries in Renaissance England database of over 17,000 books, which transcribes book-lists produced between the beginning of the sixteenth century and the middle of the seventeenth century; a few others are listed in the Cambridge probate inventories from the same period.[44] Books in PLRE include:

Ammianus Marcellinus, *Roman History* [PLRE 4.8, 277.40]

Bolton, *Foure last Things* [PLRE 255.6, 260.6, 273.1]

Bucholtzer, *Index chronologicus* [PLRE 3.88]

Cyprian, *De cænâ domini* [numerous PLRE entries]

Eucherius [PLRE 73.160, 214]

---

[43] See Dennis Flynn, 'Donne's *Ignatius His Conclave* and Other Libels on Robert Cecil', *John Donne Journal* 6 (1987): 170-72.
[44] Of the nearly 20,000 volumes listed in the inventories in *Books in Cambridge Inventories: Book-Lists from Vice Chancellor's Court Probate Inventories in the Tudor and Stuart Periods*, ed. E. S. Leedham-Green, 2 vols. (Cambridge: Cambridge University Press, 1986), only Bucholtzer, Ammianus Marcellinus, Anselm, Cyprian, Jerome, Matthieu, and Petrarca can be found in the Cambridge probate inventories.

Erasmus, ed. *De contemptu mundi* [PLRE 257.27]

Helwig, *Theatrvm historicvm* [PLRE 4.54, 260.15, 274.148]

Jerome, *Opera* [numerous PLRE entries]

Jerome, *Vitae sanctorum patrum* [PLRE 93.22, 113.7, 127.176]

Maffei, *Commentariorvm vrbanorum Raphaelis Volaterrani* [PLRE 162.35]

Manilius, *Astronomicon* [PLRE 3.60, 127.18]

Marcellus Palingenius, *Zodiacus vitæ* [numerous PLRE entries]

Petrarca, *Opera* [numerous PLRE entries]

In other words, most of these books are quite rare; finding several in the same location seems an unlikely prospect: even the vast library of Sir Thomas Browne had only five of them.[45] Christ College, Brecon, established by Henry VIII at a former Dominican friary in 1541, was close at hand, but as William

---

[45] Only Ammianus Marcellinus's *Roman History*, Helwig's *Theatrvm historicvm*, Jerome's *Opera*, Manilius's *Astronomicon*, and Petrarca's *Opera* can be found in *A Catalogue of the Libraries of Sir Thomas Browne and Dr Edward Browne, His Son: A Facsimile Reproduction*, ed. Jeremiah Finch (Leiden: Brill, 1986).

Barker observes, large and well-organized school libraries did not exist in Britain until the later seventeenth century.[46]

This leaves three institutional libraries to consider. A trove of books could be found some forty miles away at the Cathedral Library in Hereford that would have given Vaughan access to some of the books he needed. The library in Vaughan's time would have been a haven for scholars. When the medieval library was moved into the Lady Chapel in 1590, new cases were built and chains provided with which to tether the books. These bookcases were also provided with a 'writing table' or desk that allowed readers a place to work.[47] By 1630 the collection had risen to over 600 volumes, which included standard works of patristics and contemporary Protestant theology, as well as works of history, geography, and general scholarly interest.[48] Even patristic texts were readily available, as David Pearson shows in his study of the libraries of English bishops of the early seventeenth century: 'Although the reformers are always well represented, this is not to the exclusion of medieval devotional writers or to more contemporary Roman Catholic authors.'[49] Moreover, at Hereford, 'the cathedral library remained virtually untouched

---

[46] William Barker, 'School libraries (c. 1540 to 1640)', in *The Cambridge History of Libraries in Britain and Ireland, Volume I, to 1640*, ed. Elisabeth Leedham-Green and Teresa Webber (Cambridge: Cambridge University Press, 2006), 136.

[47] Joan Williams, 'The Library', in *Hereford Cathedral: A History*, ed. Gerald Aylmer and John Tiller (London: Hambledon Press, 2000), 518.

[48] Williams, 520–21. See also *The Cambridge History of Libraries in Britain and Ireland, Volume I, to 1640*, ed. Elisabeth Leedham-Green and Teresa Webber (Cambridge: Cambridge University Press, 2006), 394–95.

[49] See 'The Libraries of English Bishops, 1600–40', *The Library*, 6 (1992), 229.

in the Lady Chapel for the whole period' of the Interregnum.[50] In this cathedral city on the Welsh border, Vaughan thus could easily have taken refuge to work and found some of the books he needed (but only some).

> Anselm, St. *Divi Anselmi Cantvariensis archiepiscopi, theologi svo tempore praestantissimi, atqve celeberrimi, Omnia qvae reperiri potvervnt opera tribus distincta tomis.* Cologne, 1572–73. 2°.
>
> Bucholtzer, Abraham. *Abrahami Bucholceri, ad annum epochae Christianae 1598.* Basil, 1611. 2°.
>
> Cyprian, St. *Opera.* Geneva, 1593. 2°.
>
> Helwig, Christoph. *Theatrvm historicvm et chronologicvm.* Oxford, 1662. 2°.
>
> Jerome, St. *Opera omnia.* Cologne, 1616. 2°.
>
> Maffei, Raffaelo 1455–1522. *Commentariorvm vrbanorum Raphaelis Volaterrani.* Basil, 1544. 2°.
>
> Matthieu, Pierre. *The history of Lewis the Eleventh vvith the most memorable accidents which happened in Europe during the two and twenty 224went of his raigne.* London, 1614. 4°.
>
> Petrarca, Francesco. *Opera quae extant omnia.* 4 vol. Basil, 1581. 2°.

Most of these are folio in format, secured in the Cathedral Library through chains; quartos or octavos, though, could not be easily chained and so often disappeared. It is not

---

[50] Sheila Hingley, 'Ecclesiastical Libraries', in *The Cambridge History of Libraries in Britain and Ireland, Volume II, 1640–1850*, 124.

unreasonable to assume that some of the other books Vaughan used have simply gone missing.

Another library may have been available to Vaughan at the Cwm or Come, the Welsh Jesuit College of St. Francis Xavier in the small village of Llanrothal, Herefordshire on the border with Monmouthshire, some thirty miles from Llansantffraed. The community of Jesuits in the 'college' (an administrative term for a district with a secure annual income) of St. Francis Xavier served a large, recusant population.[51] In Vaughan's time there were as many as fourteen Jesuits resident in the Cwm. Recent research now shows that the library was comprised of at least 350 volumes.[52] In the aftermath of the Popish Plot of 1678, the Cwm came under attack when it was raided by the authorities and its volumes were confiscated and removed to Hereford Cathedral Library where some of them may still be found.[53] The sheer number of Jesuit sources Vaughan used commends the Cwm library as a possibility:

> Anselm, St. *De felicitate sanctorvm.* Ed. Jean-Baptiste Machault, SJ, ed. Paris, 1639. 8°.
>
> Bisselius, Johannes. SJ. *Icaria.* Ingolstadt, 1637. 24°.
>
> Cabilliau, Baudouin, SJ. *Epigrammata selecta.* Antwerp, 1620. 12°.

---

[51] Thomas M. McCoog SJ, 'The Society of Jesus in Wales: the Welsh in the Society of Jesus, 1561–1625', *Journal of Welsh Religious History*, 5 (1997): 1–29.

[52] Hannah Thomas, 'The Society of Jesus in Wales, c.1600–1679: Rediscovering the Cwm Jesuit Library at Hereford Cathedral', *Journal of Jesuit Studies*, 1 (2014): 572–88.

[53] For an account of the raid on the Cwm, see Herbert Croft, *A Short Narrative of the Discovery of a College of Jesuits, at a Place called the Come, in the County of Hereford* (London, 1679).

Eucherius, St. *De Contemptu Mundi*, ed. Héribert Rosweyde, SJ. Antwerp, 1621. 12°.

Ferrari, Giovanni Baptista, SJ. *Flora, sive De florvm cvltvra libri IV*. Rome, 1633. 8°.

Nieremberg, Juan Eusebio, SJ. *De arte voluntatis*. Lyon, 1631. 8°.

Paulinus, St. *Opera*, ed. Héribert Rosweyde, SJ. Antwerp, 1622. 8°.

Sirmondus, Jacobus, SJ, ed. *Sancti Valeriani episcopi Cemeliensis homiliæ XX*. Paris, 1612. 12°.

While none of these survives in Hereford today, all were in small formats and hence were vulnerable to loss during the confiscation in 1678.[54]

Henry Vaughan could have gained entrée to Cwm through family connections in two ways. He was a descendant of the third son of Sir Roger Vaughan, who was knighted for his heroism at Agincourt and whose coat of arms is incised on his gravestone in Llansantffraed: three boys' heads couped at the shoulders with a snake entwined about their necks. This branch of the family had its seat at Tretower. His grandfather, William Vaughan (*d.* 12 June 1617), had married Frances, daughter of Thomas Somerset, third son of the second Earl of Worcester.[55] The Somersets were steadfast benefactors and protectors of the Jesuits in the seventeenth century. A second, perhaps even stronger link to the recusant community in Wales came through

---

[54] The Cwm library did have a copy of St. Cyprian's *Opera* (Cologne, 1617), which is in Hereford today.

[55] See, F. E. Hutchinson, *Henry Vaughan: A Life and Interpretation* (Oxford, 1947), 5.

cousins who descended from the second son of old Sir Roger, the Vaughans of Courtfield, who also gave financial assistance, patronage, and shelter to the Jesuits.[56] Several became Jesuits and served within the College of St. Francis Xavier of Cwm, including a Thomas Vaughan (1607–75) and William Vaughan (1644–87), who was appointed as the first rector of the College after 1678, suggesting a position of some authority within the administration at the time of the raid and closure.[57] The manor at Courtfield (now in Herefordshire but formerly in Monmouthshire) was one of several missionary bases within the area and used as an emergency base following the raid in 1678. The Vaughan family's motto, *Duw a Digon* (God is Sufficient), has been inscribed within several volumes in the library, but it is not clear from existing evidence if these volumes were donated from family collections in the area, or if they were inscribed while being used in the library.[58] Unfortunately, we have no way of knowing the full extent of the Cwm library before its confiscation. Large collections such as the Hereford Cathedral Library chained books in folio but quarto or octavo volumes could not be easily chained and so often wandered. As Hannah Thomas's study of the Cwm library has shown, 'The majority of the surviving books were printed throughout the period of the most intensive Jesuit missionary work in Wales, from 1595 until 1676: it is reasonable to assume that relatively new books were being purchased on the continent and smuggled into Wales

---

[56] Theophilus Jones, *A History of the County of Brecknock*, 2nd edn. 2 vols. (Brecknock: Blissett, Davies, 1909), II, 193.

[57] See Thomas M. McCoog SJ, *English and Welsh Jesuits 1555–1650*, 2 vols. (Southampton: Catholic Record Society, 1994, 1995), II, 319; and Geoffrey Holt, SJ, *The English Jesuits 1650–1829: A Biographical Dictionary* (Southampton: Catholic Record Society, 1984), 253–54.

[58] See Hannah Thomas, 'The Society of Jesus in Wales', 588.

throughout this period.'[59] Thus it is quite conceivable that some of the Jesuit books Vaughan consulted came from nearby Cwm.

A crosscheck with the library of the Jesuit mission in Derbyshire, at the College of the Immaculate Conception at Holbeck Hall, reveals what might have gone missing from Cwm. When the Holbeck library was similarly confiscated in July 1679 in the wake of the Popish Plot and given to Sion College, London, a detailed catalogue was compiled by the librarian who received the books, which has been now fully transcribed and contextualized by Hendrik Dijkgraaf.[60] As Dijkgraaf reminds us, 'Ignatius of Loyola had stipulated that in the Jesuit colleges the students should first of all receive a solid training in the humanities.'[61] Accordingly the Holbeck Catalogue included a sizable collection of classical literature as well as a number of humanistic texts. About seventy works of Greek and Latin poets and thirty works of contemporary *belles lettres* made the journey from Nottinghamshire to London, yet not a single work of this kind can be found of the Cwm Library in Hereford today.[62] Could this *absence* be the signifier of the likely *presence* of belletristic works that might have appealed to the literary tastes of the liberators? These could have included the Jesuit works that Vaughan used for his notes and commentary.

The last possibility were libraries at Oxford though it was more than hundred miles from Newton. Vaughan's ties to Jesus

---

[59] Thomas, 'The Society of Jesus in Wales', 578.
[60] Hendrik Dijkgraaf, *The Library of a Jesuit Community at Holbeck, Nottinghamshire (1679)*, Libri Pertinentes (Tempe: Arizona Center for Medieval and Renaissance Studies, 2003), provides an annotated catalogue.
[61] Dijkgraaf, 306. He also surveys a number of treatises on seventeenth-century library theory to demonstrate the care with which Jesuit libraries were stocked with a wide range of texts (231–36).
[62] Dijkgraaf, 306–10.

College were somewhat remote at the time he was actively translating and editing, with new family circumstances adding further complications. Sometime after the end of the first phase of the war he married Catherine Wise, daughter of Richard and Lucy Wise of Gilsdon Hall, Coleshill, Warwickshire, most likely in 1646; they had four children, Lucy, Frances, Catherine, and Thomas. This means he had a very young family when he was at work on his translations in the early 1650s; at this same time, he seems also to have suffered a serious illness.[63] Moreover, conditions in interregnum Oxford were inhospitable. Having been the royal seat during the first civil war and defiant of Parliamentary authority in the second civil war of 1648, Oxford was subjected to three Parliamentary visitations through 1652.[64] These purges replaced most of the heads, professors, and fellows (including his twin brother) at Jesus College which was especially riven with controversy.[65] Only gradually in the 1650s did some degree of normality return. Accessing the collection also posed difficulties. Thomas Bodley had stipulated that senior graduates and bachelors of arts with two years standing could read in the library; later statutes allowed undergraduates so long as they showed deference to their seniors. As Charles Benson points out, gaining admission was no small feat: 'Provision for undergraduate use was not generally part of a university library's remit: indeed access by anyone other than senior

---

[63] See *Works*, 357.
[64] See Blair Worden, 'Cromwellian Oxford', in *The History of the University of Oxford*, Vol. IV: *The Seventeenth Century*, ed. Nicholas Tyacke (Oxford: Oxford University Press, 1997), 733–36.
[65] Thomas Richard, 'The Puritan Visitation of Jesus College, Oxford', *Transactions of the Honourable Society of Cymmrodorion* (1922): 1–111.

SCINTILLA 23

members of the university was often difficult.'[66] We do know that Vaughan had access as an undergraduate and sang its praises in his poem 'On Sir Thomas Bodley's *Library; the Author being then in* Oxford'; we also have an anecdote told by his kinsman John Aubrey, who remarked in a letter to Anthony Wood that Vaughan was still in possession of a Welsh grammar written by John David Rhys, *Cambrobrytannicæ Cymraecæue linguae institutions et rudimenta* (1592) 'stolen' by his brother. Referring to the book itself, Aubrey said: "Twas in Jesus college library Oxon. And my cosen Henry Vaughan [Olor Iscanus] had it in his Custody.... I have sent to Henry Vaughan, for it.'[67] To prevent such pilfering, Bodley required curators to record the names of borrowers of volumes too small to be chained (quartos and octavos) in entry-books, some of which still survive.[68] While not complete, these entry-books tell an interesting story, for between 4 February 1648 and 20 September 1649, a 'M^r. Vaughan' of Jesus College made twenty-eight visits to the Bodleian Library to work.[69] Because

---

[66] Charles Benson, 'Libraries in University Towns', in *The Cambridge History of Libraries in Britain and Ireland, Volume II, 1640–1850*, ed. Giles Mandelbrote and K. A. Manley (Cambridge: Cambridge University Press, 2006), 114. I. G. Philip and Paul Morgan, 'Libraries, Books, and Printing', in *The History of the University of Oxford*, IV, 669, note that 'Non members of the university might be admitted if they were likely to be men of influence or benefactors.'

[67] Bodleian Library MS Aubrey 8, fol. 11r; *Brief Lives*, 529. In another letter to Wood dated 10 January 1686 (Bodleian Library MS Wood F.45, fol. 192r; *Brief Lives*, 1453), Aubrey claimed that 'Thomas Vaughan [Eugenius Philolethes] stole [it] out of Jesus college Library, and Henry Vaughan (his brother haz it).'

[68] I. G. Philip and Paul Morgan, 672. These entry-books show that an average of fifteen readers ordered thirty books a day.

[69] See Bodl. Library Records, e.544: fols. 12r (4 February 1648), 12v (7 February 1648), 13r (8 February 1648), 14r (14 February 1648), 14v (16 February 1648), 15v (21 February 1648), 16v (24 February 1648), 17r (29 February 1648), 18r (7 March 1648), 18v (9 March 1648), 25r (20 April 1648), 29v (17 May 1648), 40v (20 July 1648),

the entry-books did not record folios, these entry-books by nature are incomplete; thus, 'M[r]. Vaughan' no doubt consulted many large format volumes that were not recorded.

Hitherto we have had very little real information about the activities of Thomas Vaughan in the 1640s. Aside from Henry's hazy memory most of that decade is a blank: Henry wrote Aubrey that 'my brother continued there [Oxford] for ten or 12 years [i.e., 1638-1650], and (I thinke) he could be noe lesse than M[r]. of Arts', which is partly confirmed by the dedicatory epistle to his first published work as 'Oxonii 48.'[70] Hutchinson assumed that Thomas spent much of his time in Oxford during the 1640s, neglecting his duties as rector (evicted on 22 February 1650).[71] We now have confirmation of his activities in Oxford late in that decade, for on 4 February 1648 one 'M[r]. Vaughan' of Jesus College was reading Traiano Boccalini's *The New-found politicke: Disclosing the secret natures and dispositions as well of priuate persons as of statesmen and courtiers* (London, 1626). This same quarto was also requested on 7, 8, 14, and 17 February 1648 (the only book consulted on multiple occasions by this patron).[72] This call for a second reformation based on Christian charity is the first English translation of Boccalini's *Ragguagli di Parnaso*, a chapter of

---

[41r (21 July 1648), 41r (24 July 1648), 42v (31 July 1648), 47v (2 September 1648), 49r (16 September 1648), 49v (18 September 1648), 63v (8 February 1649), 64r (13 February 1649), 74v (23 May 1649), 75v (27 May 1649), 77r (9 June 1649), 78v (15 June 1649), 78r (18 June 1649), 81v (11 July 1649), 97r (20 September 1649). Special thanks to Emily Montford for help obtain these data.

[70] 15 June 1673 Letter to Aubrey, in *Works*, 800. *Anthroposophia Theomagica* was published in London by Humphrey Blunden in 1650 under the pseudonym Eugenius Philalethes.

[71] Hutchinson, *Life*, 93.

[72] Bodl. Library Records, e.544, fols. 12r, 12v, 13r, 14r, and 14v, indicate that '4° H. 4. Ar:' was ordered, which is the shelf mark for the Boccalini's *The New-found politicke*.

which had previously appeared in German as *Die Allgemeine und General Reformation, der gantzen weiten Welt* published with the *Fama Fraternitatis, Deß Löblichen Ordens des Rosenkreutzes, an alle Gelehrte und Häupter Europæ geschrieben* (Kassel, 1614). Thomas Vaughan was certainly interested in the Rosicrucians, for he dedicated his first work to them – *Illustrissimis, et vere Renatis Fratribus R. C.* ('the most illustrious and truly reborn brothers of the rosy cross') – and a few years later brought out the first English edition of *The Fame and Confession of the Fraternity of R: C:* to which he contributed a long preface.[73] Thus it seems clear that the 'M^r. Vaughan' of Jesus College was Thomas who worked regularly at the Bodleian between February 1648 and September 1649, who would later dedicate *Lumen de Lumine* (1651) to '*my* Deare mother, *the most famous Universitie of* Oxford' with a Latin poem 'In Summum Virum *Thomam Bodleium* Equitem Auratum, *Bibliothecæ* Oxoniensis Structorem Magnificum.' The other books he consulted were mostly alchemical, such as Gerard Dorn's *Clavis totius philosophiæ chymisticæ* (Herborn, 1594 in 8°), Senior Zadith's *Tabula chymica* (Frankfurt, 1605 in 8°), Raymond Lull's *Praxis universalis* in Zetzner's *Theatrvm chemicvm* (Strasbourg, 1602 in 8°), and Arnald de Villanova's *Rosarium philosophorum sive pretiosissimum donum Dei* (Strasbourg, 1630 in 8°) – most of which he would later cite in his alchemical notebook.[74]

---

[73] *The Fame and Confession of the Fraternity of R: C* was published by Giles Calvert in 1653. On the Rosicrucian treatises, see Donald R. Dickson, *The Tessera of Antilia: Utopian Brotherhoods & Secret Societies in the Early Seventeenth Century* (Leiden: Brill, 1998), 18–19, 207–18.

[74] See Thomas and Rebecca Vaughan, *Aqua Vitæ: Non Vitis: Or, The radical Humiditie of Nature: Mechanically, and Magically dissected By the Conduct of Fire, and Ferment*, ed. and tr. Donald R. Dickson (Tempe, AZ: Arizona Center for Medieval and Renaissance Studies, 2001).

None of the books needed for the annotations in Henry Vaughan's prose annotations, however, was consulted at this time (1648–1649). Unfortunately, no other entry-books (partial or whole) survive from the period when Henry was working on his translations other than Bodl. Library Records e.544. The previous entry-book covered 1632–1640, and the following one began in 1708. So there is a huge gap in the records. There is no documentary evidence then that Henry used the Bodleian for his research (and many obstacles stood in his way), yet we know his twin brother made ample use of the library's riches. Of the thirty works needed for Henry's scholarly annotations, all but three are listed in the *Catalogus impressorum librorum bibliothecæ Bodleianæ* prepared by Thomas Hyde (1674).[75] Had he been able to work for extended periods of time at the Bodleian, he thus would have had all the necessary access. Based on the evidence of the generous bequests made to the surviving children of both Catherine Vaughan and Lucy Vaughan in the wills of their parents, it seems likely that Henry Vaughan's family remained in contact with their cousins and grandparents at Gilsdon Hall in Coleshill; so a visit to Oxford could have been made in tandem with a stay in Warwickshire. We also know that he visited his brother in London, since Thomas tells us about a 'great glass full of eye-water, made att the Pinner of Wakefield, by my deare wife, and my sister Vaughan, who are both now with god.'[76] In laying out the way from St. David's to London, Richard Grafton's *Abridgement of the Chronicles of Englande* gives the

---

[75] Works by Bisselius's *Icaria*, Grünpeck's *Speculum naturalis coelestis*, and Torriano's *Select Italian Proverbs*.
[76] *Aqua Vitæ: Non Vitis*, 244 (fol. 106ᵛ).

path Vaughan would have traveled on the principal highway, a former Roman road, to these three libraries:[77]

from Brecknoke to Hay	x. mile
[modern distance to Hay-on-Wye: 15.8 miles]	
from Hay to Harford	xiiii. Mile
[modern distance to Hereford: 21.5 miles]	
from Harford to Rose	ix. Mile
[modern distance to Ross-on-Wye: 17.5 miles]	
from Rose to Glocester	xii. Mile
[modern distance: 17 miles]	
from Glocester to Cicester	xv. Mile
[modern distance to Cirencester: 20 miles]	
from Cicester to Farington	xvi. Mile
[modern distance: 18.9 miles]	
from Farington to Abington	vii. Mile
[modern distance: 14.7 miles]	

Given what we know of the scarcity of these books, their availability in one location makes Oxford an attractive possibility for at least some of the research.

The final alternative is that Vaughan possessed some of these books himself, and there is ample evidence that he had a personal library. We know he had copies of his brother's works, for he was able to give specific details about their publication to Aubrey in 1673 – e. g., 'printed by Mr. Humphrey Blunden att the Castle in Corn-hill' or 'printed for William Leak att the Crowne betwixt the two temple-gates in fleet street' – that could only come from having them before him as he wrote.[78]

---

[77] Richard Grafton, *Abridgement of the Chronicles of Englande newly and diligently corrected, and finished the last of October, 1570* (London, 1570), fol. 204ᵛ.
[78] For details, see *Works*, 801.

We also know he had a medical library containing many quite rare volumes:[79]

> Bayle, François. *Tractatus de apoplexia* (The Hague, 1678). Bound with it are also Bayle's *Institutiones physic ad usum scholarum accomodatæ* (The Hague, 1678); *Problemata physica et medica. In quibus varii veterum & recentiorum errores deteguntur* (The Hague, 1678); and *Dissertationes medicae tres* (The Hague, 1678).
>
> Fontcyn, Nicolaas. *Commentarius in Sebastianum Austrium, medicum cæsareum: De puerorum morbis* (Amsterdam, 1642).
>
> Fonteyn, Nicolaas. *Responsionum & curationum medicinalium liber unus* (Amsterdam, 1639).
>
> Grube, Hermann. *De arcanis medicorum non arcanis commentatio* (Copenhagen, 1673).
>
> Hippocrates. *Aphorismi Hippocratis facili methodo digesti cum ipso textu . . . & Appendix, De materia medica*, ed. Johannes Tilemann (Marburg, 1650).
>
> Höchstetter, Johann Philipp. *Rararum observationum medicinalium decades sex* (Frankfurt and Leipzig, 1674).
>
> Höfer, Wolfgang. *Hercules medicus; sive, Locorum communium liber* (Nuremberg, 1675).
>
> Lotichius, Johann Peter. *Consiliorum et observationum medicinalium libri VI* (Stockholm, 1644).

---

[79] For details, see *Works*, 821–23, and Donald R. Dickson, 'Henry Vaughan's Medical Library', *Scintilla*, 9 (2005): 189–209.

Paulli, Simon. Παρεκβασις, *seu Digressio de vera, unica, ac proxima causa febrium* (Strasbourg, 1678).

Paulli, Simon. *Quadripartitum botanicum de simplicium medicamentorum facultatibus* (Strasbourg, 1667–8).

Pecquet, Jean. *Experimenta nova anatomica* (Paris, 1651).

Peyer, Johann Conrad. *Parerga anatomica et medica, septem.* (Amsterdam, 1682).

Sinibaldi, Giovanni Benedetto. *Geneanthropeiae sive De hominis generatione decateuchon* (Frankfurt, 1669).

Thoner, Augustin. *Observationum medicinalium, haud trivialium, libri quatuor* (Ulm, 1651).

Verzascha, Bernhard. *Observationum medicarum centuria* (Basel, 1677).

None of the private libraries listed in *PLRE* contains a single copy of these fifteen titles except the ubiquitous Hippocrates. Sir Thomas Browne owned only two.[80] When Vaughan died, most of these Latin volumes were acquired by Dr. William Logan, a practising physician in Bristol, either by auction or through a bookseller; and there may have been others that were lost. At his own death, Logan's books were sent to America and became incorporated into the Loganian Library, which forms one of the cornerstones of the Library Company in

---

[80] Browne owned works by Pecquet and Höchstetter. See Finch's *A Catalogue of the Libraries of Sir Thomas Browne and Dr. Edward Browne*.

Philadelphia.[81] It is reasonable to assume that Vaughan had a similar collection of literary, historical, and theological texts that would likewise have been sold at his death. The many allusions to poems by Herbert, Randolph, Cleveland, Denham and other contemporary poets can hardly have been from memory. Recently, an edition of the letters of St. Ignatius, Bishop of Antioch, bearing Vaughan's signature on its title page, was discovered in the Salisbury Library at Cardiff University, that confirms the existence of this other collection.[82] An inscription on the verso, not likely in Vaughan's hand, records the book as a gift (*ex dono*) of Vaughan:

> Sum ex Libris H. Vaughan in Regione Silurum
>
> verbi Ministri: ex dono Patris Domini
>
> Henrici Vaughan, M. D.
>
> Anno Christi:–92°.

> Pium est agnoscere per quem profecisti.

---

[81] Edwin Wolf, 'Some Books of Early English Provenance in the Library Company of Philadelphia', *The Book Collector*, 9 (1960):282. William Logan's kinsman, James Logan, was William Penn's secretary and an early benefactor of the Library Company; William's books were incorporated into the collection. See Edwin Wolf, '*At the Instance of Benjamin Franklin*': *A Brief History of the Library Company of Philadelphia*, rev. ed. (Philadelphia: Library Company, 1995), 31–36.

[82] *S. Ignatii martyris; Epistolae genuinae ex Bibliotheca Florentina*, ed. Isaac Vossius, 2nd ed. (London, 1680). The classmark is WG30 (1680). A fragment of a letter bearing his subscription has been attached to the flyleaf: 'Your Lordships most / humble servant / Henry Vaughan.' This letter no doubt conveyed the book as a gift, which would explain the origin of Vaughan's Latin motto. I would like to thank Elizabeth Siberry and also Special Collections and Archives, Cardiff University Library for their assistance.

[I am from the books of Henry Vaughan of the region of the Silures, a minister of the word: by the gift of the Father Master Henry Vaughan, M.D. – It is meet to acknowledge him by whom thou hast advanced.]

The epigraph may have been adapted from Thomas's poem on the Bodleian, which ends with a similar sentiment that seems to have been a classical commonplace: '*Pium* est Agnoscere, per *Quos* profecisti' (It is right to acknowledge those by whom you have made advancement).[83] In his Preface to the *Historia Naturalis* Pliny, for example, had averred 'est enim benignum (ut arbitror) et plenum ingenui pudoris fateri per quos profeceris' (it is, in my opinion, a pleasant thing and one that shows an honourable modesty, to own up to those who were the means of one's achievements).[84] While this edition of St. Ignatius's letters *ex Libris H. Vaughan* does not in itself constitute a library (and postdates the translations he made in the 1650s), it shows that there were others that were lost or destroyed.[85] Thomas may well have been the conduit for books of this sort, as he was likely the source for the work used for the medical translations, Heinrich Nolle's *Systema medicinæ hermeticæ generale*, for

---

[83] 'In Summum Virum *Thomam Bodleium*' in *Lumen de Lumine* (1650), B2ᵛ; in *The Works of Thomas Vaughan*, ed. Alan Rudrum (Oxford: Clarendon Press, 1984), 300, 674–75.
[84] Pliny, *Natural History*, tr. Horace Rackham, 10 vols. (Loeb Classical Library, 1940), I, 14–15.
[85] In the library of Jesus College, Cambridge is a copy of Sir Walter Raleigh's *The Historie of the World* (London, 1634) with the inscription on the recto of the front blank: 'Henricus Vaughan hunc librum tenet ex dono charissimi sui mei amici Caroli Flemen Armigeri Anno domini 1677.' This, however, is more likely a gift made to the Henry Vaughan admitted to Corpus Christi College Cambridge in 1674 by Sir Charles Flemen in 1677.

which Thomas served as 'publisher' and for which he provided a preface.

Vaughan's Greek and German

One last contribution to his scholarly editing is Vaughan's renewal of his school-boy knowledge of Greek. Before 1654 he had produced three volumes of verse and seven prose treatises – i.e., in *Poems* (1646), *Silex Scintillans* (1650), *Olor Iscanus* (1651), and *The Mount of Olives* (1652) – without a word in Greek, despite the fact that three of the prose translations in *Olor Iscanus* (1651) were from Greek originals. He translates Plutarch's *Of the Benefit we may get by our Enemies* and two short treatises, both called *Of the Diseases of the Mind and the Body* (one by Plutarch and the other by Maximus of Tyre) using a Latin edition edited by John Rainolds in which there was no Greek. [86] Yet beginning with the translations in *Flores Solitudinis* (1654), he supplies nearly a score of Greek phrases taken from his source text; in the following year, in his own preface to the second edition of *Silex Scintillans* and in its coda, he uses some Greek quotations independent of any source that shows he was reading in Greek; and then again in his medical translations (in 1655 and 1657), there are some half a dozen Greek words or phrases from his source. So what led to this sudden interest?

---

[86] John Rainolds, *Orationes Duodecim; cum aliis quibusdam opusculis*, ed. Henry Jackson, 3 pts. (Oxford, 1614 [STC 20613]), *De Utilitate* is on sigs. I11^v–L1^v; L2^r–L6^r, and N4^v–N11^r. A noted controversialist and lecturer, Rainolds (1549–1607) was reader in Greek at Corpus Christi College, Oxford, but resigned his lectureship to devote himself to divinity; he later led the Puritan delegation at the Hampton Court conference in 1604 and played a principal role in the translation of the Bible promoted by King James.

One possibility is suggested in the dedicatory letter to his kinsman Sir Charles Egerton in *Flores Solitudinis*, where Vaughan explains that he has withdrawn from the bitterness of this present age into the contemplative solitude of his native Wales and now offers such 'flowers of solitude' as may be found in his volume to comfort those similarly in need. He urges a retreat from the 'Phantasmes' of this world for the certainty of the world to come for, as he puts it, '*in the Apostles phrase*, Καθ' ὑπερβολὴν εἰς ὑπερβολὴν αἰώνιον Βάρος δόξης, a far more exceeding and eternall weight of glory.'[87] Here he quotes St. Paul's Greek but uses the language of the AV to translate 2 Corinthians 4:17, which reads: 'For our light affliction, which is but for a moment, worketh for vs a farre more exceeding *and* eternall waight of glory.' Since most of the other usages of Greek have their origin in the texts Vaughan is translating (though not all), this very first instance is quite remarkable in that it demonstrates he read – or could read – the New Testament in Greek. Of equal interest may be the fact that he expected his kinsman and the readers of *Flores Solitudinis* to be able to follow. While it may be tempting to relate this newly demonstrated ability in Greek to the oft-discussed issue of his spiritual 'conversion' or renewal in the Civil War – a fervor that led him to study the New Testament in its original tongue – he had ample opportunity to do so in the works he produced at this same time, especially in the devotional treatise, *The Mount of Olives*, and did not.

So what led to this previously undemonstrated interest in Greek? It originates, I believe, from his encountering the work of the Jesuit polymath and mystic, Juan Eusebio Nieremberg y Otin (1595–1658). The evidence suggests that he refurbished his schoolboy Greek to appreciate more fully works he truly admired. Scott Hendrickson describes him as an ascetic in the

---

[87] *Works*, 370.

neo-Platonic tradition who was deeply influenced by and indebted to the legacy of Ignatius Loyola's *Spiritual Exercises*.[88] Author of some seventy-five works, he was perhaps best known for his ascetical treatise *De la diferencia entre lo temporal y eterno* (first in 1640, then in fifty-four other Spanish editions in the seventeenth century and in Latin, Arabic, Italian, French, German, Flemish, and English translations), and for his three-part *Práctica del catecismo romano, y doctrina christiana* (1640), which was widely used throughout Spain and the Americas. His other works were published in numerous Spanish editions as well as in translation. Nieremberg enjoyed an international reputation in Spain's *Siglo de Oro*. I have discussed more fully elsewhere the extent to which Vaughan knew Greek[89]; suffice it to say here that it demonstrates the seriousness with which he pursued his calling as a scholarly editor. One of the marginal notes in his biography of St. Paulinus, in which he gives the etymology of 'night-Raven' adapted from one of Paulinus's letters, makes this ability evident: '*Paulinus will have the word which is commonly used in the Latin, to be* Nicticora, *from* νυξ *and* κορή, *which signifies the apple or candle of the eye, and not from* κοραξ.'[90] While Paulinus explains that 'eò quod pupilla oculi κόρη à Græcis vocetur', Vaughan's ability to recognize that Paulinus's word

---

[88] D. Scott Hendrickson, *Jesuit Polymath of Madrid: The Literary Enterprise of Juan Eusebio Nieremberg* (Leiden: Brill, 2015), 43–50. See also the earlier monograph on Nieremberg by Hugues Didier, *Vida y pensamiento de Juan E. Nieremberg* (Madrid: Pontifical University of Salamanca, 1976).

[89] 'Henry Vaughan's Knowledge (and Use) of Greek.' *Studies in Philology*, 118 (2020): 201–24.

[90] *Works*, 506. See 'Epistola XXVI, Ad Sanctum et Amandum', *DPO*, 228–29; Epistula XXXX in *Sancti Pontii Meropii Paulini Nolani opera* (Pars I): *Epistulae*, ed. Wilhelm August Ritter von Hartel and Margit Kamptner, vol. 29, CSEL (2nd edn, Vienna: Österreichische Akademie der Wissenschaften, 1999), 347, 3–9.

κόρη could have been κόραξ (or raven) demonstrates his command of the Greek language.

There was one linguistic challenge to which he did not rise. Following a statement on the necessity of scientific experimentation in *Systema Medicinæ Hermeticæ Generale* taken from Paracelsus, Heinrich Nolle quotes the original German:

> id quod satis arguit, Hermeticorum principia esse Galenicorum fundamentis certiora: principiorum enim artium certitudo & veritas non aliunde innotescit, quam ex praxei, vt ita recte dixerit Paracelsus *præf. Defensionum*. §. 252. Was in der Arzney mit Wercken nicht probieret wirdt, das hat sein Disputation verlohren vnd gewinnet im arguiren noch minder. Non appello Hermeticos....

Vaughan did not try to translate this German sentence (What in medicine is not proved with trial has lost the debate and won in argumentation even less) in *Hermetical Physick*, which he presumably did not understand, but simply added further elaboration:

> That the Principles of the Hermetists, are more certain then those of Galen, is sufficiently verified by their performances; besides, it is a truth which cannot be denied, that the Certainty and proof of the principles of all Arts, can by no other meanes be known and I but by practise, as Paracelsus doth rightly urge *In Præfat. Defensionum*, page 252. Now all the knowledge of the *Hermetists*, proceeds from a laborious manual disquisition and search into nature, but the *Galenists* insist wholly upon a bare received *Theorie* and prescribed Receits, giving all at

adventure, and will not be perswaded to inquire further then the mouth of their leader. I call not those Hermetists....[91]

Similarly, he reproduced the title of a work by Paracelsus as *Von den Bergfrancfheiten*, instead of *Von den Bergkranckheiten,*

den Bergfrancfhe.ten.   Vaughan

von den Bergfranckheiten.   Nolle

demonstrating that he could not read the German black-letter type Nolle used.[92] To his credit, he did provide a translation of a witticism Nolle used – *Ein newer Arzt, Ein newer Kirch-hoff*: A new Physician must have a new Church-yard – though the nonsensical 'Arkt' was given for physician, a confusion caused by Nolle's use of a digraph for *tz* and the archaic spelling *Artzt*.[93]

In sum, the marginal notes and other annotations Vaughan added to his prose works display considerable erudition and critical discernment. He drew on his wide knowledge of classical as well as contemporary writers to illustrate passages

---

[91] Heinrich Nolle, *Systema Medicinæ Hermeticæ Generale* (Frankfurt, 1613), 61; Vaughan, *Hermetical Physick* (London, 1655), 4; *Works*, 647.
[92] *Systema Medicinæ Hermeticæ Generale*, 91; *Hermetical Physick*, 69; *Works*, 669.
[93] *Systema Medicinæ Hermeticæ Generale*, 112; *Hermetical Physick*, 117; *Works*, 685. Nolle also gave a Latin translation ('Nouus medicus nouum cœmiterium erigit') that aided Vaughan.

for his readers. In all of his translations he was careful to indicate the edition he used, most comprehensively in his 'Advertisement' to Eucherius's *De contemptu mundi epistola parænetica*. That he made extensive use of a specialist's library cannot be doubted. Where Vaughan acquired the necessary books is unknown, but I have argued that while he may have worked at institutional libraries in Hereford, Cwm, and Oxford – perhaps at all three – he most likely owned some of the necessary volumes. He seems also to have refurbished his schoolboy Greek to translate more adequately the works of the learned Jesuit Nieremberg. All in all, Vaughan's labours as a scholarly editor allowed him to add considerable learning to his works in prose.

MAE SWYN RHYW HEN LAWENYDD YN FAN HYN AR DERFYN DYDD
A'R GLAS FÔR DRY'R EGLWYS FACH YN YNYS NA BU'I CHEMACH

Cwyfan
by Ann Lewis

'There is the magic of some old joy here at the end of the day and the sea turns
the little church into an island of which there is none that compares'

MIKE JENKINS

Back With the Smoke

In the cinema room the big screen
is stuck on the picture of a guitar's neck.

She keeps on pointing at her head –
'It was here I know. I've lost it!'

Whatever it is she's speaking about
has been razed as if by blanket bombs.

Then, of a sudden, it's smoke
that carries her back.

Despite the aroma of lavender
released from an envelope;

we're talking about her errant kids
stealing off down gwlis for a quick one.

'I never 'it em once mind,
jest back 'ome an put t' bed!'

I imagine her sly children
and their furtive cigarettes:

she's there chiding them
in her Rhondda town.

She returns, perplexed by the room,
to a place whose name she's forgotten.

DOMINIC WESTON

Ghost of a Flea

Once I made a vow I did only once
to develop my psychic ability until I die

there are several reasons I won't go into why
likely it was a purple-covered paperback

at the time I really thought I meant it I did
but that vow is long broken now   it is

for that reason these words are empty

I think of the wings I grew for the vow
I do   the protective shields for my psyche

of the two angels who were there for me too
to protect me and who only answered to two

different names said at the same time like
RobPhil but it sounded better in my psyche

probably they're still waiting for my call

I'm lucky I've seen lots of the world I have
like tigers sharks and whales and whale sharks

it's the small ones that make me like me though
oblivious little lifers doing time unawares

a free-floating salp jelly scooped up in my palm
waiting for the rest of its ocean-going chain

a Peruvian firefly looking like a '*Locket*'

Their chaotic flights amuse the jungle they do
hitting on our glow sticks - any port in a storm

I should be the guardian for the unknowing ones
even if they will never say my once-said name

even though I know none of them will devote
themselves to psychic abilities until they die

I probably am then but then I've broken

my vow now I have

It's Just You and Me Now

Mrs Jewel undertakes her business in a darkened room
introduces each contraption on pivots, arms and rails
peers at us through glass

Always she instructs softly with pared down commands
'Lean forward, rest here' This tall man stoops to comply
he daren't prolong events

Calmness eludes him, and with ease she denudes his
eyeballs, glares directly into him with her critical light
and he starts to refract

Mrs Jewel says she might save his sight, if he complies
Her instrument rests on his face, rapidly grinds, whirs
and blinds the first side

Panic prevents her words from resolving *'I want you to…
…tip of this ear here…'*   but it's clear she has no ears
but the grey shroud of a bob

*'Can you see a green circle? Is it darker and sharper?
Or the same?'*   All he can focus on now is how to not
breathe on her, or breathe

Always so calm, always in focus, she finds it easy to play
one side against the other, he must just keep things straight
but his right eye wavers

*'Two lines, one above the other – they will come and go
that's normal – are they together or apart? Together?
Better like this, or this?'*

The right eye can't help itself, stuttering and stammering
It can hide in daylight, but in here she revels in weakness
and now pushes harder

Remember last time you could almost get to the bottom?
But he can't bring the letters together, nothing will resolve
I'm giving you a prism

Homing in on every aberration she raises up a glass dropper
'*I'm going to put dye in*' Blue light bites, more commands
'*Up, down, blink. Good…*'

He doesn't know if he can trust Mrs Jewel's camera obscura
but she is satisfied she has detected the truth in his living eyes
as no looking glass can

ISABEL BERMUDEZ

Winter Vines

A truck is parked up in the vines.
In the back: tools, wire, bits of wood.
There's an empty armchair in a field.
The sun has turned in over the ridge
beyond the cemetery wall, where cypresses
crowd stiff and tall, stand clock-still.
Moon-faced, rooted on his short, stout legs,
Rocco stands where he stood ten years ago,
give or take a row or two.
As if time only ever moves as far as the next furrow,
inches its way across, then slips an edge.
And even as a man surveys his life's work
it turns to shadow, on the rocky page, the darkening hill.

MARGARET WILMOT

Chandeliers

Moments before the curtain rose
the lights
slipped slowly up
            and up

into a dome
which seemed to grow even
as their sparkle
dimmed
to the barest glow,

gone
the second the conductor
lifted his baton.

Then later, after the applause,
as we all stood gathering
coats, scarves,
                the chandeliers

did not descend –
(like an unclosed parenthesis

they winked in a high space
discreet as stars.

I caught a subway home that night
in a bright cloud of destiny

and song
          and chandeliers

which still wink on
in rays streaming from the chink
beneath a bedroom door.

Could I have dreamed one day
a son of mine would sing?

Practising even when
he's home on odd week-ends,

        that he'd meet a singer,
            live in a house
                    that sings.

The passing years score rings
    within rings
        within more years

while beyond thought as breath

Leporello flings
a thousand and three notes rising
out into a world of stars.

Seasonal Variation on a Railway Platform

Darkening berries on the hawthorn
thread a sombre key. The nettles dull,
have lost their sting of green. Chill
in the coming dusk signals
ground-frost.
An apple drops.

Things are falling away, given
that space –
    before pressing in again.

Was it March when pink-and-white
draped a willow bough, lured the eye past
thickening bands of leaf?
A stifled apple-tree was crowding
toward the day –

and still that urge glistens in
the swell of bark revealed
as leaves thin.

The red light winks, bell clangs.

A beaded arc flings over
the dying bramble. Rose-hips.

CHRIS DODD

The Field

is soft platinum in blue-black silhouette. By the fringe of shade,
horses stamp in moonlight. Flick through your childhood, then on,
until it's overgrown with tall, hormonal grass. Tonight, for once,
it's close-cropped and luminous, calm, just a few neural sparks.
You want to walk it, tread through what's possible, feel it, hear it
round your feet. The ground is all silver. You could grow so much
if you choose. Break off a small lump – that fine porosity, the scent
of puffball, field mushroom, electric on the tongue.

SAM ADAMS

from *'Notes of an Interview with Michel Eyquem, Seigneur De Montaine'*

I am tenderly compassionate towards
the afflicted and easily weep in company,
no matter what the occasion. For me,
nothing brings on tears so readily
as the tears of others, be they true or feigned.
I am barely moved by the sight of the dead;
rather I envy them. But I am deeply affected
by the dying. Even executions I cannot look upon
with an unmoved eye.

I am not ashamed to say, such is the childish
tenderness of my nature, that I cannot refuse
my dog's eagerness to go hunting,
even out of season. I hardly ever take live creatures
that I do not return to the fields. Pythagoras
bought fish from fishermen, and birds
from birdcatchers, to set them free.

....

The diversity of customs in different nations
does not animate me, other than with the pleasure
of their variety. Every custom has its reasons:
dishes may be of pewter, wood or earthenware,
meat on them boiled or roasted, with butter
or oil (of nuts or olives), hot or cold –
it's all the same to me. When, not in France,
I am asked if I would like to be served
in the French way, I laugh at my hosts.
I place myself at tables thick with foreigners
and rarely meet manners not the equal of our own.

JONATHAN WOODING

from 'Force'

IV.

It is Elijah, *who does not wear the armour
of the lie*. Though force may threaten to be sole
hero, its petrifactive dominion is
unloved by this candle flame, an upright sail
on a stooped and ragged wick, thinning
what force invites me to call *prophetic* darkness.
All is apparition, rightly understood!
This wind-battered garden, its staying put.

The blackbird conniving flight between blasts.
Over here you'd be forgiven for welcoming
shoots breaching soil's surface, brave whales' mouths.
How do they do it, the rooks, high up,
barreling through diaphanous water chutes?
There are limits to what cannot be thought –
Ludwig's *Tractatus*, four point one, one, four –
there are limits, Elijah; you'd be the first to say.

And these *particular point-masses* –
(forgive me) six point three, four, three, two –
not germination, flight, wind force, but rather
quick-witted blackbird, scandalous candle,
bulbs prophesying flower, the rooks high winding –
well, these, Eli, these cannot be gainsaid,
can they? The penetrable impenetrable.
Or, let me repeat after you, *Ephphatha*

K.E. DUFFIN

Visitation at Newport

Earth to paradise: Did you drop this
scarlet varlet with swatch of ultramarine
riding its back, fringed by turquoise?
Golden maned like a tiny, Horus-beaked lion,

its pebble-patterned tail drags a proclamation
behind an entire paint store, a spectrum
on fowl's kegs... Oh, come on.
It can't be real. It's from where angels strum

their lyres amid celestial fires, smitten
by the divine, and here it's stalking away in snow,
having been mistaken for a pile of hats and mittens,
a fantasia with a saffron, jet-seeded eye that says *Follow*.

A Red Golden Pheasant, aberrant glory
in the dead of winter. *Memento* minus the *mori*.

ROSIE JACKSON

Resurrection

after Stanley Spencer, 'The Resurrection: Reunion', 1945

And suddenly they are streaming back from the dead,
unburying themselves,
their tombstones mere props for gossip
now the final day has come.

Only this is not the last day,
but the first of an eternal summer
where loss turns back into desire,
for what can match the pleasure of a kiss
on the tongue of those grown accustomed to tasting nothing?

Nothing more glorious for those whose senses were lost
than these arms around the loved one's shoulder,
the conjugal embrace, the breasts
that never bruise with too much touching,
the heavy angels spilling out of windows and doors
to welcome them home.

This is what they dreamt of ascending to –
gardens, allotments, lamps pooling light over dinner.
This what they longed to recapture –
reaching round a chest that rises and falls,
the rapture of breath that doesn't stop.

Flesh ripe with joy now they are touching again –
lovers, mothers, children, fathers, plumped-up wives –
in this light that is never switched off,
these bodies that cannot have enough of each other,
this love that is always being made.

After the Door has Opened

Hazrat Babajan, a Muslim 'Perfect Master', lived in the Char Bawdi district of Pune, India. She spent her last 24 years here under a neem tree, night and day, until her death in 1931.

Here, in San Jan Mohammad Street,
dwells she who is no longer she,
whose desire is gone, who waits
for what is already done.

She is *Hafizah* –
one who has learned the Koran by heart.
She has visited the black box at Mecca,
kissed the stone of the Kaaba,
but she chooses the holy slums of Pune,
where hunger shrivels in unshaded heat.

Women break at her feet their coconuts of prayer,
make their supplications for babies.
But she knows the gift of sorrow –
how we may learn to squeeze sugar
out of grief.

She knows walking is always backwards,
the best living a kind of erasure –
each day rubbing out the folly of what went before;
how the greatest millstone of pain
cannot grind the grain of you small enough,
the finest sieve will not make you pure.

Her hair is the white of egrets.
Her face *Gulrukh* – like a rose.
And since the time her life opened
onto the fire that gives God his heat,

she knows the deceit of daylight.

So what if she was Rabia of Basra,
who wrote pleasure in the sand?
She would rather be despised as the thief
who climbed in to steal her final blanket.
Even the best poems should not be worshipped,
but hung out like rags. Words must buckle
at the knees.

Yes, here, in San Jan Mohammad Street,
trades a stall-keeper from whom few want to buy.
Her age – a hundred or more –
small matter as she sits
under the angel of the neem tree –
seven centuries between each feather.

FRANK DULLAGHAN

Skull

There could be a day when the clogging clay
will be scraped from my skull, and
I will be eye-socket to eyeball with the future.

The only thoughts then inside that skull
will be those projected from that interrogation.

Yet here I am imagining what I might say
for myself: the obvious facts that there is no life
without death; that time is unstoppable.

But also, that inside that bone casing,
a being existed, looked out on the world, and

coloured it in – its emotional landscape,
its hints at meaning. And, of course, that other,
that future, in this imagined tableau, no less confused

about this journeying, about travelling
until the dark hides everything there is.

KEVIN CAHILL

Lao Tzu has a Go

'Those who possess all under heaven
give themselves no trouble with that end.'
— Tâo Te Ching

Tilled, deft, rivelled, spilt
yielding, skin-like piece of batik
received for my birthday morning.
A ribbed, rice-flecked, botanical,
docile and twilled sheaf of litheness
swept across my arms.
I am swept across by the piebald
ox and oxherd with huge lop-sided
flowers stealing the horizon
from people who don't care…
Their coign overlooked by slime-hung
massy jungle stretching overhead,
and cast upon solvent, unmolested loam.
A woofy, sandwiched, nameless group
of thumb-lovely, earth-plumbing people
melting along the cattle-tracks.

PATRICK DEELEY

Dream of a Fallen Beast

The behemoth from the last swallow-hole
dead now, her flanks swollen,
for all the world was still imaginable
as immaculate, resting up a while –

but the wet ditch, and behind it
the hoof-scraped mossy hill against which
she'd tried to clamber or twist,
together with sunrise and the evaporating

sheen of night's chill, bespoke
festerings to come, before again the dark
took a scraggy bite. I knew the drill,
the build towards disintegration,

but waited to hear the slow sounding out
of a constant, tuneless whistle
from some perforated part, and this came
to me as the final, eviscerate art

of one who had crowned the earth
with strangeness, with pause for wonder.
Then she, caught between
banal and fabulous, seeming hardly more

than my own twist of whimsy,
moved – not of her own steam but enough
to have me say: 'Mother." Soon
they arose, the new-born in multitudes

wriggling, spilling, glistening,
for her carcass had now metamorphosed
to edible detritus – and in a circle
in that place I saw thin-boned figures

shuffling threadbare: children
of the future, who might have been our own
forebears gathered about a great
fallen beast, dancing still, dancing to less.

Rigour

If St. Kevin feels compelled
to keep his hand held out as a branch
to accommodate the nest
a blackbird has begun to build,

a disconcerting twist is all
I can bring to the myth – of a man
who for years holds out his hand
as a sign of devotion to God

until the hand becomes locked
in place, the initial crippling pain
grows numb, the slow
shrivel commences, fingernails

resembling pale scimitars crossed
and interlaced, the hand
still required to curve, the bone
to curl – as a frond of fern

will curl – against its own extent.
The worshipper's example
of rigour, subsuming
within the sorry animal of his body

the urge to avow, to embrace
the world at large, the muddled
here and now, is one
I would not or could not follow,

who by comparison know only
that, in madcap childhood, the 'man
with healing hands'
set to rights my dislocated bones.

Yet, stooped all hours at this task,
I work a crucifixion of sorts.
too tightly battened words,
a too narrowly adhered to stance –

where I had thought to make
the craft limber as well as strong,
earth-wrought, capable
of flight, swerving the way Kevin's

blackbird or any other
might, through branches into light,
scattering glad notes from
a garden fencepost or a chimney pot.

MILES PARKER

Luggala 1982*

*I can contemplate nothing but parts, & parts are all
little! My mind feels as if it ached to behold & know
something great – something one and indivisible...*
                                         Coleridge (Letters)

Where eye sees the whole hill,
mind already finds – bush, boulder,
the syllogism of the stream.

Where eye sees the whole bush,
mind already finds – furze or fraochán,
thorn or berry, leaf and a gleaming beetle.

Where aye says the whole boulder,
mind already winds over schist or quartzite,
the crystal's grain and mica's gleam.

Where aye and ever the stream
runs over slope and boulder, one from its spring to its fall,
mind, all ready, binds cataract and chute, wave and droplet,
into rainbowed whole
and the sum of sounds into one rough soothing rush.

And all is Luggala, to the last atom,
whole, unlost, in the body's recollection,
in the mind's I.
                        (Cambridge 2019)

* Luggala, a mountain in Co Wicklow, Ireland, is pronounced 'Lugger-law', with the emphases on the first and last syllables.

B.J. BUCKLEY

Music for the Third Ear

Chromatic or
twelve tone, thrum
of living field
against

unclothed
skin – flesh, living, still
knows the small
vibrations – worm,
grub, sow bug –
makes room.

Bats and swallows
bows
for wind-strung air

breath's slip jig

last night a scream
from the slough, this morning
fox scat
rich with meat

moon's long arpeggio across
the day, the dark

and fog
over the river, wet-fingered
melodious
mute counterpoint

heart-drum's skipped

beat

one hand
on the instrument, one
turning

the page

LINDA SAUNDERS

My Mother Being Very Deaf

I put my lips right to her ear
when she was dying
behind the curtains on the ward:
the send-off

she always needed at the door,
the seal of approval, affirmation
that the visit had gone well
and she could relax now,

being loved.
I felt she would hear me
in the dunes of her dying,
where she waited between each

and the next
last breath
for my kiss of a word
in her ear.

For years it was a problem between us,
the need to repeat, shout,
misunderstanding,
humour gone flat,

but one day, inspired,
seeing her tv listener,
its mic suckered to the box,
I plucked it free

and spoke into that.
A miracle!
We could chat quietly, laugh,
as I rediscovered

her forgotten mind,
as crisp and edgy as each magnified sound,
her impatience, too quick as ever
to finish my sentences.

Now I dabbed cologne on a hanky
and held it to her temples,
remembering that cool, astringent
comfort to my childhood fevers.

Whispered goodbye,
as I might blow on a remaining spark,
believing I reached that self,
still sharp
        as a star.

ROSIE JACKSON

Resurrection

after Stanley Spencer, 'The Resurrection: Reunion', 1945

And suddenly they are streaming back from the dead,
unburying themselves,
their tombstones mere props for gossip
now the final day has come.

Only this is not the last day,
but the first of an eternal summer
where loss turns back into desire,
for what can match the pleasure of a kiss
on the tongue of those grown accustomed to tasting
nothing?

Nothing more glorious for those whose senses were lost
than these arms around the loved one's shoulder,
the conjugal embrace, the breasts
that never bruise with too much touching,
the heavy angels spilling out of windows and doors
to welcome them home.

This is what they dreamt of ascending to –
gardens, allotments, lamps pooling light over dinner.
This what they longed to recapture –
reaching round a chest that rises and falls,
the rapture of breath that doesn't stop.

Flesh ripe with joy now they are touching again –
lovers, mothers, children, fathers, plumped-up wives –
in this light that is never switched off,
these bodies that cannot have enough of each other,
this love that is always being made.

After the Door Has Opened

Hazrat Babajan, a Muslim 'Perfect Master', lived in the Char Bawdi district of Pune, India. She spent her last 24 years here under a neem tree, night and day, until her death in 1931.

Here, in San Jan Mohammad Street,
dwells she who is no longer she,
whose desire is gone, who waits
for what is already done.

She is *Hafizah* –
one who has learned the Koran by heart.
She has visited the black box at Mecca,
kissed the stone of the Kaaba,
but she chooses the holy slums of Pune,
where hunger shrivels in unshaded heat.

Women break at her feet their coconuts of prayer,
make their supplications for babies.
But she knows the gift of sorrow –
how we may learn to squeeze sugar
out of grief.

She knows walking is always backwards,
the best living a kind of erasure –
each day rubbing out the folly of what went before;
how the greatest millstone of pain
cannot grind the grain of you small enough,
the finest sieve will not make you pure.

Her hair is the white of egrets.
Her face *Gulrukh* – like a rose.
And since the time her life opened
onto the fire that gives God his heat,
she knows the deceit of daylight.

So what if she was Rabia of Basra,
who wrote pleasure in the sand?
She would rather be despised as the thief
who climbed in to steal her final blanket.
Even the best poems should not be worshipped,
but hung out like rags. Words must buckle
at the knees.

Yes, here, in San Jan Mohammad Street,
trades a stall-keeper from whom few want to buy.
Her age – a hundred or more –
small matter as she sits
under the angel of the neem tree –
seven centuries between each feather.

Review: *The Works of Henry Vaughan*, ed. by Donald R. Dickson, Alan Rudrum, and Robert Wilcher, 3 vols (Oxford: OUP, 2018). £295 hardback only.

PHILIP WEST

Since its first appearance in 1914, L. C. Martin's *The Works of Henry Vaughan* (2nd edition 1957) has remained the standard scholarly edition of Vaughan's complete works – and, indeed, the only widely available text of Vaughan's remarkable and undervalued prose works. Martin's text was edited to the highest scholarly standards of the day, and its texts have stood the test of time. Its annotations, on the other hand, are notoriously sparse, while its brief introductions offer little contextual help for the reader – not a reflection on Martin's scholarship but rather on how little had been published on Vaughan when the edition was produced. In time, supplementary commentary appeared in the form of E. L. Marilla's edition of the secular poems (1958); but it was really Alan Rudrum's edition of *The Complete Poems* (1976, repr. 1983) that provided the necessary depth and range of annotation to match Martin's textual quality, and the two editions became, together, the essential reading kit. Rudrum's notes skilfully illuminated Vaughan's literary borrowings, alchemical and hermetical ideas, and, not least, his seemingly endless remembrances of the poetry of George Herbert and of the Bible, and in doing so, opened the door to renewed scholarly interest in Vaughan in the late twentieth century.

    This triumphant new three-volume edition from Oxford University Press is intimately related to Rudrum's and Martin's achievements, but supersedes them to become the essential text

Review: *The Works of Henry Vaughan*

for future scholarly work on Vaughan. It includes all of the surviving writing: Henry's nine printed volumes, but also transcripts of the handwritten medical receipts found in his surviving books, and of his letters to John Aubrey. Alan Rudrum's continued editorial involvement means that the core of his Penguin edition of the poems is here, but all of this material has been thoroughly revised by Rudrum and his co-editors Donald R. Dickson and Robert Wilcher, from whose own expertise the edition benefits at every turn. The texts of Vaughan's works — unmodernised, but corrected where press errors crept into the seventeenth-century editions — have been divided between Volumes I and II (with the notes relegated to Volume III), where they are sensibly arranged in chronological order of publication, rather than by attempting to reconstruct the order in which Vaughan wrote particular poems – an almost impossible task given the absence of the sort of manuscript witness associated with contemporaries such as Carew and Herrick, or the self-conscious datings indicated by Milton in his *Poems* (1645). One notable result of this arrangement by date of printing is that the two parts of the expanded edition of *Silex Scintillans* (1655) are split between Vols I and Vol. II, whereas Martin's and Rudrum's editions printed them one after the other, more or less as they were in *Silex* (1655). The new arrangement has the advantage of restoring the first edition of *Silex* (1650) to its original integrity, and of highlighting the fact that Part II was written during a period of 'significant changes in the political situation in South Wales' (p. 544), a period the reader can now trace as they step through the pages from one *Silex* to another, via *The Mount of Olives: Or, Solitary Devotions* (1653) and *Flores Solitudinis* (1654). But if the edition's arrangement implicitly foregrounds the importance of historical contexts, the editors are also admirably aware of form, and of the particular modes of attention encouraged by its role in lyric poetry. Notably, they have chosen to present the poems on a 'clean page', free from notes, so that readers can first encounter the poems and prose without the intervening *'thorns* and *briars'* of annotation ('The Bee').

The Introductions and Commentary of this edition are a superb achievement, offering the reader what is, by some stretch, the most comprehensive and up-to-date picture of Vaughan's work and life. Critical introductions to individual works, including commentary on textual problems, are printed throughout Vols I and II, and will immediately become indispensable reference points. Martin's edition provided only barebone glosses, so that the reader encountering a text such as Vaughan's devotional book, *The Mount of Olives* (1652), would find only a short biographical note on the work's dedicatee, Sir Charles Egerton, but no further guidance about what lay ahead. By contrast, the new edition provides an account of how in *Mount of Olives* Vaughan constructs an alternative devotional 'rite', an analysis of his use of the day as a unit of devotion, and a discussion of sacred place – all of which provide the reader with excellent starting points from which to begin their readings. The other introductions are similarly informative and orientating. Supplementing these, Vol. I also includes a fine biography divided into sections on Vaughan's early life, military service, and medical career, and a thoroughly engaging 'History of Henry Vaughan Scholarship and Criticism' in which the fascinating story of Vaughan's reception and readership is told, really for the first time. Beginning with earliest readers, it traces his reception via the imitations of admirers in the Romantic period, through the appreciative comments of Victorian readers and editors, right up to the complex twentieth-century critical engagements that have shaped Vaughan's modern reputation. Nothing like this 'critical heritage' has really been available before, and it was a real joy to read. Scholarly reception history it may be, but I think any lover of Vaughan's work will be moved as they read

Review: *The Works of Henry Vaughan*

about the admiration his poetry has provoked in other readers across 350 years.

The entirety of Volume III (569 pages) is taken up with commentary notes. Happily everything that was useful in Rudrum's and Martin's editions has been preserved here, but newly enriched with new layers of annotation. As well as drawing on their own considerable expertise, the editors have made sympathetic and appropriate use of the work of earlier critics and writers, not least (as the flyleaf states) the pioneering work of Louise Guincy and Gwenllian Morgan, whose unpublished historical and biographical material was drawn on in F. E. Hutchinson's biographical study *Henry Vaughan* (1947). One welcome aspect of this inclusivity in the commentary is that it demonstrates the breadth of Vaughan's readership, and the wide range of critical approaches that have been used to engage with his writing. Another is that the edition gives a clearer sense of the occasional textual complexities of the early editions – for instance, exploring in detail the differences between the text of '*Isaacs* Marriage' in the first and second editions of *Silex*. Where appropriate, headnotes to the texts present helpful summaries of recent critical debates, in a similar way to Helen Wilcox's invaluable edition of George Herbert's poems (Cambridge, 2013). Such guides to critical reading will be valued by new and old readers alike, especially when used alongside the substantial bibliography (pp. 1411–1430; the very high page numbers are because the three volumes are through-numbered). While the reader familiar with Rudrum's and Martin's editions will recognise some of the annotatory material in Vol. III, there is so much more here now that I never felt I was reading a reprint. Far from it, in fact. The commentary is not only better presented and polished, but seriously revised, more informative than ever, and by far the best way into the pleasures, and the scholarly contexts, of Vaughan's writing.

Physically, the edition resembles the attractive Clarendon Press editions of the twentieth century, of which L. C. Martin's edition was an early example: navy blue hardbacks with light blue dust jackets. Within the volumes, Vaughan's intricate stanza forms are recreated by the editors as closely as possible to the original editions, while the principal of following the original compositors' italics and orthography is well justified. The books are certainly a pleasure to use, with handsome typefaces, though some readers might note that Oxford has shrunk the margins around and between poems since Martin's day. On occasion, too, Oxford's typesetting felt needlessly unsympathetic to form, letting down the excellent, and sympathetic, textual editing. Poems that might have been set on two pages are often split across three, leaving two lonely lines at the top or bottom of a page – something which sounds trifling, but such widows/orphans were straightforwardly avoided by both Martin's and Rudrum's editions, which in both cases improves the reading experience. This is a minor grumble, however, and the only moment where I winced a bit was in 'The Call' (in *Silex* I), whose second stanza is shaped somewhat like the 'glass' (i.e. an hourglass) that the speaker says he will fill with penitent tears. In Martin and Rudrum it is set on a single page and can thus be visualized by the reader, but here an unfortunate page-break cracks the glass in half!

This edition is a massive achievement and a landmark in Vaughan editing and scholarship. Anyone with more than a passing interest in Vaughan will find these volumes rewarding throughout, and in many ways a revelation. At almost £300, however, it is unlikely to find its way onto many shelves outside university libraries and specialists with deep pockets. Certainly the edition is designed first and foremost to be used as a resource for study: the reader really requires a desk and at least two hands to prop open both the volume containing the text and Vol. III containing the commentary notes. The excellence

Review: *The Works of Henry Vaughan*

---

of the editorial work here offers the perfect platform for bringing Vaughan to a wider readership again, just as Alan Rudrum's edition did in the last third of the twentieth century. A paperback edition (say, in Oxford's 'Twenty-first Century Authors' series) that reprinted just the major poetry collections, and selected but substantial chunks of the devotional prose, would be an wonderful offshoot of this magisterial *Works*.

CONTRIBUTORS

SHANTA ACHARYA is the author of twelve books; her latest publications are *What Survives Is the Singing* (Indigo Dreams Publishing, UK; 2020) and *Imagine: New and Selected Poems* (HarperCollins Publishers, India; 2017).
www.shantaacharya.com

SAM ADAMS's publications include three books of poems and the novels *Prichard's Nose* (2010) and *In the Vale* (2019), both from Y Lolfa. A third novel, *The Road to Zarauz* will appear from Parthian in July and is already available to Kindle readers.

THOR BACON's *Making the Shore* won the 2017 *Red Dragonfly Press* Chapbook Award. His recent poems appear in *The St. Katherine Review* and *The Aurorean*. More information can be found at www.ThorBacon.com

CAROL BARBOUR's poems are published by *Transverse Journal*, *The Fiddlehead*, *Acta Victoriana*, and *Canthius*. Recent books include the poetry collection *Infrangible* (Guernica Editions, 2018), and the artist book *Alter Pieces* (2019).

ALEX BARR has two poetry collections, *Letting In The Carnival* (Peterloo) and *Henry's Bridge* (Starborn). He lives in Fishguard.

MARTIN BENNETT lives in Rome where he teaches, proofreads and contributes occasional articles to *Wanted in Rome*. He was 2015 winner of the John Dryden translation prize.

ISABEL BERMUDEZ's *Madonna Moon* won the Coast to Coast to Coast Pamphlet Prize 2018. Her latest collection is *Serenade*, poems from Spain and the New World (Paekakariki Press). She has previously published *Small Disturbances* and *Sanctuary (Rockingham)* and *Extranjeros* (Flarestack Poets).

LINDA BLACK is Editor of *Long Poem Magazine*. Her collections are *Slant*, *Root* and *Inventory* (Shearsman 2016, 2011, 2008). *The Son of a Shoemaker* (Hearing Eye, 2012) about Hans Andersen was a Poetry Society exhibition. A 5th collection is forthcoming.

PATRICK BOND lives in Lewes, Sussex. A first collection was published by Paekakariki Press in 2017. *Signals on the Railway Land* comprises a yearlong immersion in nature and the metaphysical. An article and poem appeared recently in *Raceme* magazine.

TONY BROWN is Emeritus Professor of English and Co-Director of the R.S. Thomas Research Centre at Bangor University. He is the author of *R.S. Thomas* (U. of Wales P., new ed. 2013) and co-edited, with Jason Walford Davies, *Too Brave to Dream* (2016), a collection of previously-unpublished ekphrastic poems by Thomas. He is currently editing Elsi Eldridge's autobiographical journal for publication.

B.J. BUCKLEY is a Montana poet and writer who has been a teaching artist in Arts-in-Schools/Communities Programs in the western United States for more than 40 years. Her most recent book of poems is *Corvidae: Poems of Ravens, Crows, and Magpies* (Lummox press 2014).

KEVIN CAHILL is a writer from Cork. His work has appeared in recent issues of *Oxford Poetry*, *The London Magazine*, *Wild Court*, and *The Pre-Raphaelite Society Review*.

NOEL CANIN was born and raised in South Africa. She now lives in Israel where she is a translator from Hebrew to English, a BodyMind therapist and student of Hakomi Psychotherapy, and a poet. She has a son, a daughter and five grandchildren.

CLARE CROSSMAN lives outside Cambridge. She has published four collections of poetry. Her fifth from Shoestring Press is due later this year. She recently published a biography, *Winter Flowers*, about the Cumbrian artist Lorna Graves.

CLAIRE CROWTHER's first collection, *Stretch of Closures* (Shearsman), was shortlisted for the Aldeburgh Best First Collection Prize and her latest collection, *Solar Cruise* (Shearsman), is a Poetry Book Society Spring Recommendation for 2020.

NEIL CURRY's most recent collection of verse is *On Keeping Company with Mrs Woolf*. Also recent is his study of William Shenstone, the 18th century poet and landscape gardener.

SAM DAVIDSON's 'Love's Many Names' (Angelico Press) is available on Amazon.

WILLIAM VIRGIL DAVIS's most recent book of poetry, his sixth, is *Dismantlements of Silence: Poems Selected and New*. His first book, *One Way to Reconstruct the Scene*, won the Yale Series of Younger Poets Prize. His poetry has been published worldwide.

HOLLY DAY's poetry has recently appeared in *Asimov's Science Fiction, Grain,* and *Harvard Review*. Her newest poetry collections are *Where We Went Wrong* (Clare Songbirds Publishing), and *Into the Cracks* (Golden Antelope Press).

PATRICK DEELEY is a poet, memoirist and children's writer from Galway. His seventh collection with Dedalus, *The End of the World*, was shortlisted for the 2020 Farmgate National Poetry Award. He is the recipient of the 2019 Lawrence O'Shaughnessy Award.

DONALD DICKSON is professor of English at Texas A&M University. He is the author of numerous studies on the Vaughans, including a critical edition of Thomas's *Aqua Vitæ: Non Vitis* and *The Works of Henry Vaughan* (with Alan Rudrum and Robert Wilcher). He is a Fellow of the Royal Historical Society and a founding editor of *Scintilla*. He is editing the *Letters of John Donne* (forthcoming OUP).

CHRIS DODD lives in the Lake District. *Feeding out the Rope*, a pamphlet of his poems, is published by Smiths Knoll.

K.E. DUFFIN's work has appeared in *Agni, Canary, The Carolina Quarterly, Clade Song, Kestrel, The Moth, Salamander, Scintilla (18, 21), Slant, Southern Poetry Review*, and other journals. *King Vulture*, a book of poems, is published by University of Arkansas Press.

FRANK DULLAGHAN is an Irish writer who at the time of writing was locked down in Kuala Lumpur, Malaysia. He has four collections published by Cinnamon Press, most recently *Lifting the Latch* (2018).

ANNA FLEMING writes on environment, ecology and adventure. She grew up in mid-Wales and now lives in Scotland where she is writing her debut book, *Time on Rock: A Climber's Route into the Mountains* (forthcoming with Canongate in 2022).

ROBIN FORD is a native of the Isle of Wight; its land and seascapes strongly influence his writing. His poems have appeared in a wide range of magazines, and he has had three collections published.

ROGER GARFITT's latest collection is *The Action* (Carcanet, 2019). His memoir, *The Horseman's Word,* is a Vintage paperback and a CD of Poetry & Jazz, *In All My Holy Mountain*, is available from:
www.restringingthelyre.wordpress.com

SAM GARVAN has had work published in anthologies and journals including *The North, Poetry Salzburg Review, Thorax,* and *Iota.* He has a Ph.D. from London University and works for a London beekeeper.

TOM GOUTHWAITE grew up in Yorkshire. He is a natural scientist and keen apprentice of the unknown with only a few poems published to date. He is grateful to Roger Garfitt for guidance at Madingley Hall Masterclasses.

MARC HARSHMAN's *Woman in Red Anorak* (Lynx House Press, 2018) won the Blue Lynx Poetry Prize. His fourteenth children's book, *Fallingwater...,* was published by Roaring Brook in 2017. He is co-winner of the 2019 Allen Ginsberg Poetry Award.

MARTIN HAYDEN lives in Suffolk. Since 2007 he has had several spells on Iona, as a volunteer with the Iona Community. His pamphlet of Iona poems, *Good Ground Beneath My Feet*, is out now from The Garlic Press, who are also bringing out his first collection later this year.

MICHAEL HENRY has been widely published in magazines including recently in Acumen, Tears in the Fence and The

North. He has published four collections with Enitharmon Press and one with Five Seasons Press.

JEREMY HOOKER's most recent publications are *Ditch Vision: Essays on Poetry, Nature, and Place* (Awen, 2017), and a sequence of prose poems, *Under the Quarry Woods* (Pottery Press, 2018). He has completed a new collection of poems (*Word and Stone*), and is finishing a book of essays on poetry, painting, and photography (*Art of Seeing*). He is an emeritus professor of the University of South Wales.

RIC HOOL's 10th collection of poetry, *Personal Archaeology*, published in May 2020 by Red Squirrel Press, is thematically centred on Cullercoats & Northumberland, his home for many years.

ROSIE JACKSON's books include *Two Girls and a Beehive: Poems about Stanley Spencer and Hilda Carline Spencer* (Two Rivers Press, 2020) and *The Light Box* (2016). She won 1st prizes in Poetry Space 2019, Wells 2018, Cookham 2017. www.rosiejackson.org.uk

MIKE JENKINS is a retired comprehensive school teacher living in Merthyr Tydfil. He has co-edited *Red Poets* magazine for 27 years and edited a recent anthology of radical poems from Cymru 'Onward/Ymlaen!' (Culture Matters).

FRANCES-ANNE KING lives in Bath. Extensively published in national and international journals, *Weight of Water* (Poetry Salzburg) was published in 2013, *From Palette to Pen,* an Anthology, in 2016. She won 1st prize in the Oxford SciPo Competition (2018).

PETER LIMBRICK is an educationalist interested in babies who have neurological impairment. He aspires to a Buddhist view of birth and death.

SARAH LINDON's poems have appeared in *Agenda, Magma, Orbis, Oxford Poetry, Poetry Wales, Scintilla, South, Stand, The Frogmore Papers, The Interpreter's House* and *The Reader*. She has an MPhil in Writing from the University of Glamorgan, and lives in London.

PAUL MATTHEWS helps students in the Storytelling course at Emerson College in Sussex to write creatively. His most recent gathering of poetry is *This Naked Light*, available from Troubador books, or from the author: paulmatthewspoetry.co.uk

EDMUND MATYJASZEK was born in London and now lives in the Isle of Wight. He has two collections of poems: *Walsingham, England's Nazareth*; and *The Rosary: England's Prayer* (St Paul's Publishing). His poetry and playwriting have won numerous awards.

SEAN H. MCDOWELL is Associate Professor of English and Director of the University Honours Program, Seattle University and Editor of the *John Donne Journal*. His poems have appeared in the U.K., Ireland, Greece, the United States, and Australia.

NICHOLAS MCGAUGHEY is an actor. His poetry has been published in *The Atlanta Review, Popshot, Acumen, Prole, Marble, A New Ulster, Skylight 47, The Lampeter Review, Poetry Scotland, Ink Sweat and Tears, Poetry Salzburg* and *Smith/Doorstop*.

BRUCE MCRAE is a multiple Pushcart nominated poet published in *Poetry, Rattle* and *The North American Review*. His books are *The So-Called Sonnets* (Silenced Press), *An Unbecoming Fit Of Frenzy* (Cawing Crow Press) and *Like As If* (Pski's Porch).

CHRISTOPHER MEREDITH is a novelist and poet from Brecon and Emeritus Professor at the University of South Wales. Recent work includes *Brief Lives* (short stories) and *Air Histories* (poems). New poems, *Still*, and a short novel, *Please*, appear from Seren in 2021.

HUBERT MOORE's tenth full collection was *The Feeding Station* (Shoestring Press, 2018). This is to be followed in 2021 by *Owl Songs*.

NICHOLAS MURRAY is a poet and literary biographer living in the Welsh Marches. He won the Basil Bunting Prize in 2015 and was highly commended in the 2019 Poetry London Clore Prize. His most recent collection is *The Yellow Wheelbarrow* (Melos, December 2019).

HOLLY FAITH NELSON, Ph.D., Professor and Chair of English at Trinity Western University, has published widely in the literature of the seventeenth century, most recently completing a monograph with Dr. Sharon Alker on the literature of siege warfare: *Besieged. Early Modern British Siege Literature, 1642-1722* forthcoming McGill-Queen's University Press.

ANDREW NEILSON's poems, essays and reviews have appeared in a number of journals in both the UK and the US. He is Vice Chair of The Poetry Society.

ROBERT NISBET, sometime creative writing tutor at Trinity College, Carmarthen, has been published widely in Britain and the USA. He is a recent Pushcart Prize nominee.

CHRISTINE VALTERS PAINTNER is an American poet living in Galway, Ireland. Her first poetry collection is titled *Dreaming of Stones* and her second, *The Wisdom of Wild Grace*, is forthcoming this fall from Paraclete Press. You can find her at AbbeyoftheArts.com.

MILES PARKER is half Irish and half English. He trained as a marine biologist and worked as a government science adviser in Ireland and England on environmental and food issues until he retired. He has written poetry since his teenage years.

PETER PIKE is a recently-retired Anglican priest living in mid Wales. He taught in special needs education before ordination in 1984. After twenty-eight years of predominantly rural ministry in the dioceses of Blackburn and York, he became Archdeacon of Montgomery in the Church in Wales in 2012. His doctoral thesis was entitled: 'Read poems as prayers': Seamus Heaney and Christian tradition'.

ANN PILLING won the Smith/Doorstop pamphlet competition in 2008 and has since published three more collections of poems. Her fourth, *Jigsaw*, comes out from Shoestring in October. She lives in the Yorkshire Dales which she calls 'the country of my heart.'

MARTIN POTTER (https://martinpotterpoet.home.blog) is a poet and academic, and his poems have appeared in *Acumen*, *The French Literary Review*, *Eborakon* and other journals. His pamphlet *In the Particular* was published by Eyewear in December, 2017.

RANAJIT SARKAR was born in Banagram, Bengal, in 1932, and from 1970 onwards he taught Sanskrit and Indian Cultures at the University of Groningen, The Netherlands. He was a multi-lingual writer, publishing poetry in Bengali and in French before his death in 2011. The poem included here in *Scintilla* is the first of his English poems to be published.

LINDA SAUNDERS's poems have won numerous awards including first prize at Teignmouth Festival 2019, third at Wells 2018 and first in the Second Light poetry competition 2018. Her latest book is *A Touch on the Remote* from Worple Press.

CLAIRE SCOTT is a Pushcart Prize nominated poet published in *The Atlanta Review, Bellevue Literary Review, New Ohio Review, Enizagam* and *Healing Muse* among others. Claire is the author of *Waiting to be Called* and *Until I Couldn't.*

BRIGID SIVILL has published poems in several magazines and won prizes in *Artemis* and *New Writer*. She writes in Normandy and has finished three pamphlets and a collection length full poem. She blogs at opsimathpoet.wordpress.com.

SUSAN SKINNER was encouraged by her father to read and write poetry from a young age. She has published five collections and belonged to various poetry societies. She is now part of a Zoom group who reads poems to each other online for the joy of it.

THOMAS R. SMITH has two books forthcoming in 2020, a poetry collection, *Storm Island* (Red Dragonfly Press) and *Poetry on the Side of Nature: Writing the Nature Poem as an Act of Survival* (Folded Word Press). He lives in River Falls, Wisconsin.

KENNETH STEVEN is first and foremost a poet but also a novelist, a children's author, and translator from Norwegian.

BEATRICE TEISSIER is an archaeologist and independent scholar based in Oxford.

JILL TOWNSEND lives in NE Hampshire. She has had work published in various journals, most recently *Brittle Star* and *Orbis*, and can be heard reading in the Secondlightlive archive.

DAVIDE TRAME lives in Venice; his poetry collection, *Make It Last*, was published in 2013 by Lapwing in Belfast.

DENNI TURP lives in north Wales and is a graduate and post-graduate of Bangor University. Her poetry has appeared in magazines including *Prole*, *South Bank Poetry*, *Tears in the Fence*, *Popshot* and *ARTEMISPoetry*, in several anthologies and on poetry webzines.

MAREK URBANOWICZ has been published in numerous magazines including *Agenda* and *Frogmore Papers*. He was awarded an MA in Voice Studies in 2014 by Royal Central School of Speech and Drama. He has been a qualified acupuncturist since 1979.

JOHN WELCH lives in London. His most recent collection, *In Folly's Shade*, was published by Shearsman in 2018.

PHILIP WEST teaches English at Oxford, where he is a Tutorial Fellow of Somerville College and an Associate Professor in the Faculty of English. His study of the Bible in Vaughan's poetry, *Henry Vaughan's 'Silex Scintillans': Scripture Uses*, was published in 2001. He has also published on George Herbert, Ben Jonson, John Donne, and James Shirley. His edition of Shirley's poems is forthcoming from OUP, and he is also editing one volume of *The Oxford Edition of the Sermons of John Donne*.

DOMINIC WESTON produces wildlife programmes for television, runs over Somerset hills and writes poetry. He won the 2019 Hastings LitFest Poetry Prize and has been published in *Magma Poetry, The North, Agenda, Under The Radar, Skylight 47 and Black Bough Poetry*.

CHARLES WILKINSON's poetry collections include *Ag & Au* (Flarestack, 2013) and *The Glazier's Choice* (Eyewear, 2019). He lives in Powys, Wales. More information about his work can be found at his website: http://charleswilkinsonauthor.com

MARGARET WILMOT was born in California but settled in Sussex, England in 1978. Smiths Knoll published her pamphlet *Sweet Coffee* in 2013. *Man Walking on Water with Tie Askew*, a full-length book of poems, was published by The High Window in June 2019.

JONATHAN WOODING writes for *The Friend*, and for *Cassandra Voices*. His published work is with *academia.edu*. He was awarded a PhD for *An Atheist's Prayer-Book*. He writes and lectures on Geoffrey Hill's poetry.

The Artist

ANN LEWIS, RCA, was born in St. Asaph, Flintshire, and studied at the Art College in Bangor followed by Graphic Design at Exeter College of Art and Design. After graduating in 1988, she returned to Wales, working as a freelance designer and illustrator. Gradually she evolved from designer to fine artist and was elected a member of the Royal Cambrian Academy in 1993. She was elected Vice-President of the Academy in April 2014. Since March 2009, Ann has worked as a full-time printmaker, specialising in the reduction method of linocutting. She produces limited editions of hand-printed linocuts in her studio above the Conwy Valley in North Wales. Her work is inspired largely by the Welsh landscape, its mountains, rivers, waterfalls and coastline. Ann has work in the National Library of Wales' collection, the Government's Art Collection and The Grosvenor Museum, Chester's Print Collection.

Printed in Great Britain
by Amazon